The Wireless Internet Opportunity for Developing Countries

Funding for this publication was provided by

*info*Dev Program of The World Bank

United Nations ICT Task Force

Wireless Internet Institute

United Nations
Information
and
Communication
Technology
Task Force

WIRELESS INTERNET INSTITUTE

For ongoing online updates to this book,
please visit w2i.org.

The Wireless Internet Opportunity for Developing Countries is co-published by the Information for Development Program (*info*Dev) of the World Bank; the United Nations ICT Task Force; and the Wireless Internet Institute (W2i), a Division of World Times, Inc., to build on the momentum set by the conference of the same name cohosted by the Task Force and W2i at UN Headquarters in New York on June 26, 2003.

This reference document serves as a basis for seminars and roundtable discussions to be held at the World Summit on Information Society in Geneva in December 2003 and provides a multi-annual living knowledge base with ongoing updates in both electronic and printed form.

First printed November 2003

The findings, interpretations, and conclusions expressed in this document are entirely those of the authors and the Wireless Internet Institute, and should not be attributed either to the World Bank, its affiliated organizations, or members of its Board of Executive Directors or the countries they represent; or to the United Nations ICT Task Force, its members, or subsidiary bodies.

Funding for the conference was provided by:
Intel Corporation

This book is distributed on the understanding that if legal or other expert assistance is required in any particular case, readers should not rely entirely on statements made in this book, but should seek the services of a competent professional. Neither the Wireless Internet Institute, the UN ICT Task Force nor the World Bank accepts responsibility for the consequences of actions taken by those who do not seek necessary advice form competent professionals on legal or other matters that require expert advice.

ISBN 0-9747607-0-6

Contents

UNITED NATIONS NATIONS UNIES

THE SECRETARY-GENERAL

WELCOMING MESSAGE TO "THE WIRELESS INTERNET OPPORTUNITY FOR DEVELOPING COUNTRIES" CONFERENCE
New York, 26 June 2003

It gives me great pleasure to send my greetings to the Wireless Internet Institute, the United Nations Information and Communication Technologies Task Force, and all other organizers and participants in this conference on wireless Internet opportunities for developing countries.

As you know well, the swift emergence of a global "information society" is changing the way people live, learn, work, and relate. An explosion in the free flow of information and ideas has brought knowledge and its myriad applications to many millions of people, creating new choices and opportunities in some of the most vital realms of human endeavour.

Yet too many of the world's people remain untouched by this revolution. A "digital divide" threatens to exacerbate already-wide gaps between rich and poor, within and among countries. The stakes are high indeed. Timely access to news and information can promote trade, education, employment, health, and wealth. One of the hallmarks of the information society—openness—is a crucial ingredient of democracy and good governance. Information and knowledge are also at the heart of efforts to strengthen tolerance, mutual understanding, and respect for diversity.

Wireless technologies have a key role to play everywhere, but especially in developing countries and countries with economies in transition. With considerable speed and without enormous investments, Wi-Fi can facilitate access to knowledge and information, for example by making use of unlicensed radio spectrum to deliver cheap and fast Internet access. Indeed, it is precisely in places where no infrastructure exists that Wi-Fi can be particularly effective, helping countries to leapfrog generations of telecommunications technology and infrastructure and empower their people.

For this to happen, however, we urgently need to reach a clear understanding of Wi-Fi's development potential, identify the obstacles, and develop a realistic plan of action that would bring together all stakeholders—governments, the private sector, civil society—in a coherent, synergistic, and sustainable endeavour. This conference offers a valuable forum for doing just that. Your recommendations will also help guide the work of the UN Information and Communication Technologies Task Force. I wish you every success and look forward to working with you on one of the leading development challenges of our times.

Kofi A. Annan

Acknowledgements

The publishers—the Information for Development Program (*info*Dev),
United Nations ICT Task Force, and the Wireless Internet Institute (W2i)—
wish to acknowledge the following individuals and organizations for their
contributions to "The Wireless Internet Opportunity for Developing Countries"
conference, research, and publication program.

CONTRIBUTING AUTHORS

Kofi A. Annan, Secretary General, United Nations
Amir Alexander Hasson, Founder, First Mile Solutions
Noopur Jhunjhunwala, Analyst, Wireless Internet Institute
Kevin C. Kahn, Director, Communications Technology Lab, Intel Corporation
Mohsen Khalil, Director, Global Information and Communication Technologies, The World Bank
Axel Leblois, Co-Founder, Wireless Internet Institute; President, World Times, Inc.
Peter Orne, Editor, The WorldPaper, World Times, Inc.
Alex (Sandy) Pentland, Founder, Digital Nations Consortium, MIT Media Lab
Iqbal Z. Quadir, Lecturer, Harvard's Kennedy School of Government; Founder, GrameenPhone
Theodore H. Schell, Founder, Cometa Networks

CONFERENCE STEERING COMMITTEE

Daniel Aghion, Executive Director, Wireless Internet Institute
Shiv Bakhshi, Sr. Research Analyst, Global Wireless Infrastructure, International Data Corporation
Scott Borg, Research Fellow, CDS Tuck School of Business
Jeff Giesea, Publisher, FierceWireless
Brian Grimm, Director, Marketing, Wi-Fi Alliance
Yasuhiko Kawasumi, Chairman, New Technologies for Rural Applications Group, ITU
Mohsen Khalil, Director, Global Information and Communication Technologies, World Bank
Sarbuland Khan, Director, Division for ECOSOC Support and Coordination, United Nations
Axel Leblois, Co-Founder, Wireless Internet Institute; President, World Times, Inc.
Amolo Ng'weno, Founder, Africa Online
Jeff Orr, Director, Marketing, WiMax Forum
Alexander (Sandy) Pentland, Founder, Digital Nations Consortium, MIT Media Lab
Bimal Sareen, Former CEO, Media Lab Asia; International Consultant
Alan Scrime, Chief, Policy and Rules, Office of Engineering and Technology, FCC
Khaldoon Tabaza, Founder, Arab Advisor
Sriram Viswanathan, Managing Director, Strategic Investments, Intel Capital
Linda Wellstein, Partner, Wilkinson Barker & Knauer, Llp.

CONFERENCE FACULTY

Talal Abu-Ghazaleh, Vice Chairman UN ICT Task Force; CEO, TAGI

Lisa Agard, Executive Vice President, Cable & Wireless

Daniel Aghion, Executive Director, Wireless Internet Institute

Shiv Bakhshi, Sr. Research Analyst, Global Wireless Infrastructure, International Data Corporation

Scott Borg, Research Fellow, CDS Tuck School of Business

Bill Carney, Board Member, Wi-Fi Alliance

Amir Dossal, Executive Director, United Nations for International Partnerships

Pat Gelsinger, Chief Technology Officer, Intel Corporation

Vic Hayes, Sr. Scientist, Agere Systems

Mohsen Khalil, Director, Global Information and Communication Technologies, The World Bank

Sarbuland Khan, Director, Division for ECOSOC Support and Coordination, United Nations

Ed Malloy, USAID

Alex (Sandy) Pentland, Founder, Digital Nations Consortium, MIT Media Lab

Robert Pepper, Chief, Plans and Policy, FCC

Iqbal Quadir, Lecturer, Harvard's Kennedy School of Government; Founder, GrameenPhone

Bimal Sareen, Former CEO, Media Lab Asia; International Consultant

Theodore H. Schell, Founder, Cometa NetworksMohammad Shakoury, Board Member, WiMax Forum

Jabari Simama, Executive Director, Atlanta Mayor's Office of Community Technology

Francisco Vieira, Operational Specialist, IT4D, Inter-American Development Bank

Sriram Viswanathan, Managing Director, Strategic Investments, Intel Capital

Linda Wellstein, Partner, Wilkinson Barker & Knauer, Llp

FIELD PRACTITIONERS

Dileep Agrawal, CEO and Co-Founder, WorldLink ISP

Michael Best, Board Member, SARI Project

Christopher Clark, Co-Founder, Amazon Association

Robert Freeling, Executive Director, Solar Electric Light Fund

Amir Alexander Hasson, Founder, First Mile Solutions

David Jarvis, Founder, UniNet Communications

Rafiqullah Kakar, National Project Coordinator, ICT4D, UNDP-Afghanistan

Paul Meyer, Founder, Internet Project Kosovo; Co-Founder, CEO, Voxiva

Margery O'Donnell, Project Administrator, John W. McCormack Graduate School of Policy Studies, UMass Boston

Paul Shaw, CEO, Africa-Online

Sharron Tate, Co-Founder and Director of Operations, Baja Wireless

Lee Thorn, Chairman and Founder, Jhai Foundation

Randy Zadra, Managing Director, Institute for Connectivity of the Americas

CONFERENCE SHOWCASE PRESENTERS

Intel Corporation
Nomadix
Radiant Networks, Plc.
Telesym, Inc.
Tropos Networks
Vivato, Inc.

UNITED NATIONS ICT TASK FORCE

Sarbuland Khan, Director, Division for ECOSOC Support and Coordination, United Nations
Sergei Kambalov, Deputy Executive Coordinator
Samuel Danofsky, Program Manager
Maria Lehtinen, Special Assistant to the Director
Enrica Murmura, Media and Outreach Officer
Daniella Giacomelli, Program Manager
Julianne Lee, Senior Policy Advisor to the Chairman
Linda Sanchez, Administrative Assistant

INFODEV

Bruno Lanvin, Program Manager
Jacqueline Dubow, Program Coordinator

EDITORIAL ADVISORY BOARD

Bruno Lanvin, Program Manager, *info*Dev
Jacqueline Dubow, Project Coordinator, *info*Dev
Sarbuland Khan, Director, Division for ECOSOC Support and Coordination, United Nations
Sergei Kambalov, Deputy Executive Coordinator, UN ICT Task Force
Theodore H. Schell, Founder, Cometa Networks
Peter Orne, Editorial Director, W2i

W2i EDITORIAL AND PRODUCTION TEAM

Daniel Aghion, Project Manager
Keith Frazier, Art Director
Noopur Jhunjhunwala, Analyst
Axel Leblois, Contributing Editor
Christine Leblois, Project Administrator
Peter Orne, Editorial Director

Preface

THE PROMISES OF WIRELESS INTERNET TECHNOLOGIES have generated much interest on the part of the international-development community. While in developed nations these technologies have primarily been associated with mobility applications and local area networking in homes and offices, their most intriguing application in developing nations is the deployment of low-cost broadband Internet infrastructure and last-mile distribution.

The rationale for such interest is simple in theory: The digital divide cannot be resolved any time soon because of the prohibitive cost of deploying conventional wired infrastructure in developing countries. Wireless Internet, however, has the potential to solve this bottleneck, as the collection of articles and case studies in this volume demonstrates. And leading IT vendors do confirm that wireless Internet should be the most promising accelerator of technology adoption in developing nations. In support of these hopes, technology is readily available and more accessible every day thanks to standardization and fast-declining costs.

So, why should this topic become central to the World Summit on Information Society initiative?

First, wireless Internet may be a very effective and inexpensive connectivity tool, but it does not carry any magic in itself. It can only be successfully deployed as demand for connectivity and bandwidth emerges in support of relevant applications for the populations served. These may be supporting e-government, e-education, e-health, e-business or e-agriculture applications. But those are not easily implemented in the developing world.

Demand aggregation for wireless Internet connectivity around applications that make sense in support of wireless infrastructure investment is the first important challenge that the UN ICT Task Force, *info*Dev, and the Wireless Internet Institute wanted to explore and document. The authors of this compendium have investigated dozens of field experiments around the world and selected several that exemplify some of the innovative approaches to this challenge. They do suggest that wireless Internet can indeed be sustainably and in some cases profitably deployed in support of economic and social development objectives in developing countries.

One common characteristic of these case studies is their unconventional, often grass-roots origin. Entrepreneurs from the private, public, or not-for-profit sectors have independently developed original deployment models pointing to potential solutions for the developing world. Most, however, must confront serious challenges that are nontechnical in nature and associated with legacy regulations, administrative obstacles, and the opposition of incumbent telecommunications operators.

This book attempts to clarify the key issues that need attention on the part of governments, international development agencies, and nongovernmental organizations whose goals are to bridge the digital divide. It is a first step only and will be complemented by further updates and analysis. Documenting this worldwide phenomenon, sharing best practices and experiences, and promoting adequate policies can help to accelerate the resolution of the many obstacles that constrain the expansion of one of the most promising information-technology tools of this century. ◑

Executive summary

The *Wireless Internet Opportunity for Developing Countries* examines the emergence and promise of proven and inexpensive technologies to bridge the connectivity gap at the root of the digital divide. It brings together the perspectives of thought leaders from the fields of social and economic development, information and communication technology, government, regulation and international standards; and the examples, collected in a case-study compendium, of wireless Internet field practitioners at work throughout the developing world.

When affordable and relevant, information and communications technologies have been adopted at a fast pace within developing countries, leapfrogging traditional infrastructure. Following the fast growth in developing countries of cellular telephones over fixed lines—in Africa, the ratio is approaching 2 to 1—Internet applications supporting telecommunications as well as economic, education, and social services activities have proliferated rapidly. In Brazil, for example, 90 to 95 percent of tax returns are now filed online, a far greater percentage than in North America. Connectivity and the information access it brings unleashes human capital and increase productivity and knowledge sharing in underserved areas where it has been most constrained.

New wireless Internet technologies are ready to fulfill this promise, supported by universally accepted standards set by the Institute of Electrical and Electronics Engineers (IEEE) for both wireless local area networking (the 802.11 standards known as "Wi-Fi") and long-distance point-to-point connectivity (the 802.16 standards known as WiMax). A multitude of devices, software, and services on the market are designed to inter-operate with unified protocols in the frequency spectrums defined by these standards.

In recent years, the definitions of unlicensed spectrum have normalized around two major sets of frequencies: the Instrument, Scientific, and Medical band (ISM) at 2.4 Ghz; and a newer allocation in the 5-Ghz to 6-Ghz range adopted by the World Radiocommunication Conference (WRC) in June 2003. More and more devices are reaching the market with chip sets that will allow the instant detection and connectivity to local hotspots where they are available.

Developing countries, however, are presented with a number of technological trade-offs. For example, in the absence of wired infrastructure, wireless point-to-point connection can be used very effectively to provide inexpensive broadband access. But online interactive applications and voice-over IP require as little "latency" as possible. As the number of hops grows along a connection, so does latency. And so-called multiple-hops configurations will often end up in a common link to a high-performance fiber backbone, presenting yet another potential bottleneck. Developing countries will need to establish a minimum level of performance based on the capacities of local infrastructure.

Fast declining costs promise to make wireless broadband more and more affordable, especially as it is embedded in more devices, including "intelligent phones" and other hardware that is able to automatically shift from a local 802.xx connection with voice-over IP to a regular cellular service. Perhaps more important for developing countries is new "smart" technology under development that will help to optimize spectrum use by automatically limiting interference, solving a potentially difficult issue in dense areas.

Equally intriguing for developing countries is new technology allowing users to automatically relay radio signals, which creates a "mesh network" of wireless connections that could develop a life of its own, reducing the number of required base stations. This technology lowers the cost of infrastructure while increasing the cost to users only marginally, and provides welcome connectivity redundancy in dense areas.

Because many developing countries are advanced in the adoption of wireless cellular telephony, the topic of the future convergence between IEEE 802.xx standards and cellular standards of the International Telecommunication Union (ITU) is obviously important. The 802.16 standard, or WiMax, was defined for broadband distribution to fixed points on reasonably large-channel allocations, whereas mobile telephony standards are designed to transport voice on narrow bands. Both, however, are evolving toward each other's position: 802.16e supports some form of nomadic applications while 3G, with a high level of mobility, offers mid-bandwidth data services. 4G and 802.20 may still be at the conceptual level, but developing countries will need to remain well informed in order to optimize existing infrastructure, given that these technologies will continue to evolve.

Amid the fast pace of technological advance, regulatory authorities are faced with a number of issues. Defining international unlicensed bands in support of wireless Internet and other applications has been long and arduous, but the process has come to fruition thanks to the active role of several key constituents including the US Federal Communications Commission, the European Union, the ITU, and the IT industry. The 2003 World Radio Conference decision to allocate the 2.4-Ghz and 5-Ghz bands to license-exempt applications, as voted on by participating countries, was a landmark for future universal adoption. Today, 41 percent of developing countries have regulations supporting license-exempt bands, compared with 96 percent among developed countries. And many developed countries, including the United States and the European Union, have regulations that now support the commercial use of license-exempt spectrum.

One of the issues among developing countries is the delicate transition from telecom monopolies to free competition and a deregulated environment. Legacy infrastructures, old regulations, lack of competition, the wish to preserve monopolies' cash flows, and political issues related to control over information all contribute to the slow the adoption of new regulations supporting license-exempt bands and their free use for commercial purposes.

Even where license-exempt bands are authorized, additional regulations still limit its use. Some countries impose license fees on individual equipment for hotspots and access devices. In the absence of a clear regulatory framework supporting competition in telecommunications, access to an Internet backbone may be made either impossible or cost-prohibitive by incumbent telecoms or through licensing by regulatory authorities.

In this context, voice-over IP is perceived as potentially disruptive and has triggered forceful opposition from the governments of many developing countries. For the purpose of bringing wireless Internet to underserved areas, however, VoIP may play a very positive role in providing inexpensive telephone access and helping local wireless Internet service providers to benefit from higher traffic.

The IT industry views the June 2003 decision of the World Radio Conference as a long-term positive impact, opening an unlimited field of opportunities—a win-win on a worldwide basis for service providers, hardware and software companies, and most importantly customers.

Today's wireless economics are already compelling: Wireless local loops are about one third the cost of copper or fiber land-line service, while packet-based broadband computer networks cost one ninth of land-line service. Ease of set-up, use, and maintenance are affordable for both users and providers. Tests in rural settings show that a $30 wireless PC card can provide good connectivity up to a half-kilometer radius with line-of-sight and up to 20 kilometers with antennas and repeaters. And Wi-Fi access points can be purchased for $80.

Developing basic asynchronous services may be the best starting point for rural connectivity, including voice messaging, e-mail, and batch downloading.

MIT Media Lab researchers have developed and demonstrated a combination of wireless technology and asynchronous delivery that brings the cost of asynchronous Internet service by two orders of magnitude below land-line expenses. These observations suggest that developing-country governments should adopt regulatory frameworks that support independent wireless Internet service providers and that do not restrict voice-over IP applications.

The inspiring mobile-telephony success story of GrameenPhone in rural Bangladesh shows how entrepreneurial villagers can be recruited to adopt a technology that provides them greater connectivity and therefore economic opportunity on a whole new scale. GrameenPhone has built the largest cellular network in the country, in numbers of subscribers, with investments exceeding $300 million and a subscriber base of more than one million. Its rural program is available in more than 35,000 villages, providing telephone access to millions while fostering a generation of village micro-entrepreneurs. GrameenPhone is an example of how widespread connectivity can dramatically unleash human potential and increase productivity. The model may be applicable with limited variations to wireless Internet services that generate local employment and ownership.

Experienced industry leaders, however, point to the many obstacles encountered by start-up wireless Internet service providers in developing countries. These include operating in areas with low disposable income, low initial demand for wireless services because of a small PC base, difficulty aggregating local demand, and limited financing options. A primary question, therefore, is how the revenue/cost equation is solved. Moreover, despite favorable regulations and stated support for ISPs, incumbent telecoms may create significant hurdles with predatory pricing, untenably high bandwidth rates, denial of interconnections for long periods, delays in repairing leased lines, or failure to meet contractual levels of services. Similar issues are encountered in developed countries, but in developing countries ISPs have less economic and legal leverage.

Case studies of field deployments of wireless Internet networks raise the many issues discussed above in a multiplicity of operating environments. In the run-up to the UN ICT Task Force and Wireless Internet Institute conference held at UN Headquarters on June 26, 2003, dozens of case studies were gathered, of which twelve are collected here to showcase some of the variation in operating environments, sizes, business models, and purpose.

Whether motivated primarily by development objectives, for profit, or by the challenges of deployment, the field practitioners in these pioneering case studies share the goal of bridging the digital divide using broadband wireless technology. Each found a unique solution for overcoming roadblocks.

The case studies analyzed for this compendium appear in five categories revealing core aspects of wireless broadband deployments in developing countries:

▶**Remote Regions** provide the harshest environmental test of the technology and of the implementation models (pp. 43-50).

▶**Wireless Internet Service Providers** are primarily driven by profit but can also contribute to regional development (pp. 53-66).

▶**Shared Access** provides connectivity to regions that cannot afford individual access (pp. 69-76).

▶**Adaptive Technologies** rethink off-the-shelf solutions to overcome local limitations (pp. 69-85).

▶**Rebuilding Nations** can draw from the models above to rebuild a communications infrastructure and jumpstart social and economic development (pp. 89-95).

While examining these case studies, analysts of the Wireless Internet Institute confirmed key analysis offered by experts on a more "macro" level:

▶In most areas, there is simply no wired alternative available either for geographic and social environment, economic, or maintenance reasons.

▶Most case studies show early adopters innovating as they set-up their network.

▶Inter-connection equipment and service to a backbone are a major expense.

▶In remote areas, power supply remains a difficult issue.

▶Explaining the benefit of broadband and getting the "buy-in" of local communities is crucial and demand aggregation is often necessary, including through community centers or kiosk models.

► When people connect to the Web, they want to communicate, and e-mail and voice and video mail are the most popular uses of wireless broadband networks in the developing world.

► The Internet's biggest advantage over other communication technologies is that it can provide an array of solutions and products for e-governance, e-health, e-education, and e-commerce.

► Incumbent telecom operators in the developing world guard their terrain carefully. Rural areas are marginal markets for incumbents, so entrepreneurs may face few initial barriers, whereas in cities, the entrepreneur is likely to face the incumbent and regulatory authority head on.

► Different responses to these entities, however, present varying risks. Some operators choose to directly confront telecom operators and authorities, lobbying against them domestically and internationally, which can lead to confiscations, project termination, and even criminal charges. Others bypass the regulatory environment altogether when the authority is not too aggressive. Still others engage in the bureaucratic process, seeking required permissions and even trying to form alliances with incumbents.

► Authorities may be more convinced by projects with a social-development outcome.

Local governments are encouraged to develop a greater awareness of the potential benefits of wireless Internet connectivity, to foster local initiatives, and carefully adjust their regulatory frameworks, taking into account worldwide standards, barriers to competition, local Internet backbone access conditions, and the monitoring of early wireless Internet experiments.

Entrepreneurs and field practitioners looking for resources or simply seeking assessments of industry and technology trends will find an analysis of the wireless Internet value chain followed by a directory of firms and technologies. For ongoing online updates to this book, visit and contact the Wireless Internet Institute at w2i.org. ◖◗

The wireless Internet opportunity for developing countries

By Mohsen Khalil

WHEN IT COMES TO WIRELESS TECHNOLOGY, I do not believe we're going to see the usual classical behavior, where there will be a technology transfer from the industrialized world to the developing world. There may actually be a reverse flow of innovative solutions, and the developing world might in fact dictate the standards and bring many solutions to the global market.

At the World Bank, our interest is in achieving connectivity access and trying to devise solutions in the developing world, regardless of what the technology platform is. If we see an opportunity in a specific technology, we'll take it, but that is not the object itself. We truly believe there is a direct link between access and poverty reduction. In the developing world, access presents an unprecedented opportunity for people who have been disconnected from the global economy.

One project in Bangladesh, which was partly financed by IFC, has been very successful. GrameenPhone has surpassed the incumbent and worked well in an inefficient, regulated environment to bring cellular telephony to rural areas. Women in the villages did this by providing community solutions and services, and many on average earned double their income per capita.

Another example of how access provides opportunity is the provision of online information to farmers, so they can watch for lower costs and improve their profit margins. And yet another example is Novica, the largest portal enabling artisans in rural areas to sell their products abroad— for example, to department stores in the United States. The World Bank has just provided them with an equity investment.

In a broader way, IT can provide a much more efficient platform for the delivery of social services and health and education. One of the imperatives for creating a proper investment climate and improved economic growth is improved government and transparency. In Brazil today, for example, 90 to 95 percent of all tax returns are done online, which, in comparison, is much higher than in the United States. IT also helps people, from NGOs to interest groups, to be able to connect to the global community and voice their rights.

Unlike the industrial or agricultural revolutions, where you needed huge amounts of capital to operate, once you provide information access, you have the power to unleash the potential of human capital no matter where you are.

Perhaps the Internet bubble hasn't served us well, because people thought about this revolution in the context of stock markets. I do not believe it's over, however. It's a dormant volcano that will come back again. It allows an opportunity to enter the global market, it allows improved efficiency throughout the value chain, and ultimately it's going to have an impact on the political texture of any society. For example, coverage of the war in Iraq wouldn't have been the same; you couldn't have access to information. None of what happens in the world today would have been the same twenty or thirty years ago. ◍

Mohsen Khalil is Director of the Global Information and Communication Technologies Division of the The World Bank.

GLOBAL CONNECTIVITY RISING

TELEPHONE SUBSCRIBERS, WORLD, MILLIONS

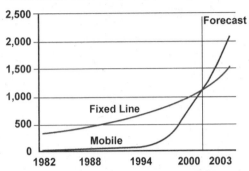

MORE MOBILE COUNTRIES

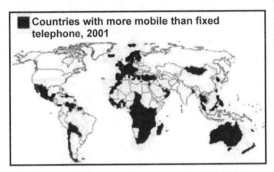

Countries with more mobile than fixed telephone, 2001

Note: In the left chart, 1982-2001 is based on real data; 2002-2003 on projections. In the right chart, 97 countries that are shaded had more mobile users than fixed lines, as of year-end 2001.
Source: ITU World Telecommunications Indicators Database.

Global connectivity is on the rise, thanks largely to cellular technology. In 2001, the number of fixed lines and the number of cellular lines crossed. Since then, we have had more mobile phones than fixed lines. The growth rate of mobiles is significantly higher than fixed lines. The blue dots on the map show all the countries and regions where there are more mobile phones than fixed lines. Today, there is more mobile telephony in developing countries than in industrialized countries.

INTERNET GROWTH SLOW BUT SURE

INTERNET USERS, WORLD, MILLIONS

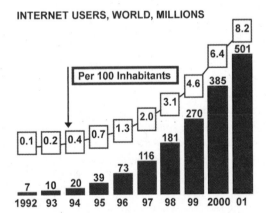

COUNTRIES CONNECTED TO THE INTERNET

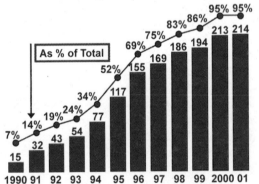

Note: In the right chart, countries refer to 225 countries or territories. 'Connected refers' refers to the establishment of a direct link to the internet enabling it to be accessed by a local telephone call
Source: ITU World Telecommunications Indicators Database

Although it has mostly been concentrated in the industrialized world, there has been an explosion in Internet growth. You can see almost exponential growth in Internet users, and in almost every single country today there is some form of Internet connectivity.

BRIDGING THE DIVIDE

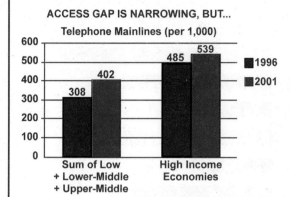

ACCESS GAP IS NARROWING, BUT...

Telephone Mainlines (per 1,000)

- Sum of Low + Lower-Middle + Upper-Middle: 308 (1996), 402 (2001)
- High Income Economies: 485 (1996), 539 (2001)

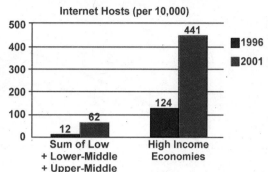

...INFORMATION GAP WORSENSFOR SOME

Internet Hosts (per 10,000)

- Sum of Low + Lower-Middle + Upper-Middle: 12 (1996), 62 (2001)
- High Income Economies: 124 (1996), 441 (2001)

The access gap is narrowing, but the information gap is widening. In terms of telephone connectivity, the gap between the high-income countries and the middle-income countries is narrowing. But if you measure the gap by connectivity of Internet hosts, the gap is widening in a very serious way.

INTERNET ACCESS GAP ENDURES

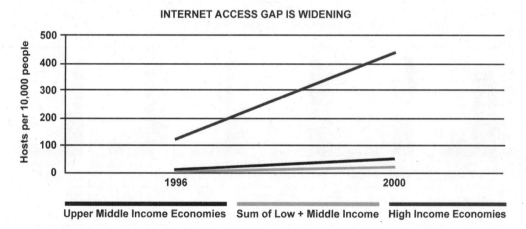

INTERNET ACCESS GAP IS WIDENING

Hosts per 10,000 people

— Upper Middle Income Economies — Sum of Low + Middle Income — High Income Economies

The Internet access gap is widening, which is very concerning. Although the gap has been narrowing among regions of the developing world, access has been concentrated in the 10 largest economies. There are serious gaps between different regions. For example, the gap between East Asia and South Asia is huge. There are huge gaps between rural and urban (improving somewhat) and between the educated versus not educated.

THE TRIUMPH OF MOBILE

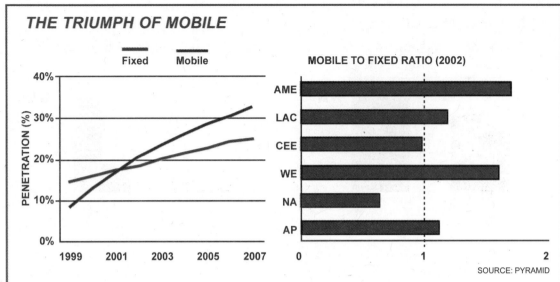

— Fixed   — Mobile

MOBILE TO FIXED RATIO (2002)

SOURCE: PYRAMID

The growth rate of mobile phones is expected to be significantly higher than fixed-line growth. We're approaching a point where for every fixed line in Africa, we have two cellular lines, at least. If you compare this with North America, it's the opposite.

LDC'S ARE MAKING GAINS

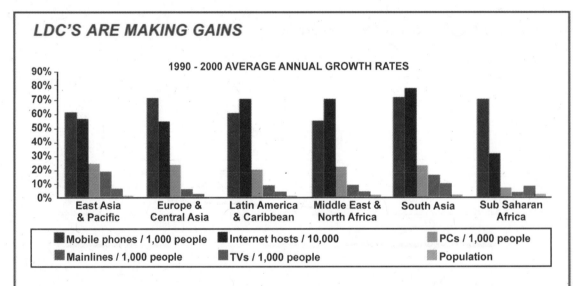

Among the Least Developed Countries, we have experienced a 50- to 70-percent compounded rate of growth for mobile phones on an annual basis. That's great news. Much more was done in the past 10 years than over the previous 50 years, and much more can be done, but the challenge is how to do it. On the Internet, though the growth rate is high, we're starting from an extremely low base.

TECHNOLOGY PRIMER

On spectrums and standards, architecture and access points

By Kevin C. Kahn

WIRELESS TECHNOLOGY IS REVOLUTIONIZ-
ing the way in which PCs, PDAs, and
other similar devices access the Internet
at high speeds. This is happening both in the last
100 meters where it provides a mobile alternative
to Ethernet, and in the longer-reach access networks where it complements technologies like
DSL and cable modems. This primer provides a
technical overview of the various wireless technologies currently or soon to be in use, how and in
what spectrum they operate, and where they each
fit in a larger Internet-access architecture.

Basic Spectrum Issues

The radio spectrum is used by a wide variety of
users ranging from consumer radio and television,
to weather and aircraft radar, to data communications. Ranges of frequencies are assigned to various uses based on history, technical properties of
the various frequencies, and other considerations.
Because radio waves do not respect national bor-
ders, international agreements attempt to harmo-
nize uses across multiple countries where conflicts
could occur or where there is benefit using common equipment. For this primer, we are interested
in the use of frequencies for short- to medium-
range data communications.

To control how various bands are used, national
regulations have commonly required licenses for

Kevin C. Kahn is an Intel Fellow and Director
of the Communications and Interconnect
Technology Lab, Corporate Technology Group,
Intel Corporation.

operators to be permitted to use particular frequencies. Licensed bands, or radio channels, are most
important to relatively high-power and longer-range
uses of radio where significant chance of interference between different radio users would exist if
control is not exercised. For example, TV channels
are allocated so that multiple broadcasters do not
operate so near to one another that receivers would
see their reception garbled.

For some types of radio use, requiring licenses is
too cumbersome, so many national regulators have
also defined unlicensed or license-exempt bands.
To maintain order in such bands, there are generally rules limiting the power and other technical
properties that a radio operating in the bands can
use. Because of the typical low power used, users
are expected to be able to use such bands either
without mutual interference or by managing any
interference among themselves without governmental legal help.

The most commonly discussed unlicensed
band, available virtually worldwide today, is in the
vicinity of 2.4 GHz. This band is often called the
Industrial, Scientific, Medical (ISM) band because
its initial allocation was to allow radio emissions by
various sorts of equipment. This is the band that is
being used today for Wireless Local Area
Networks (WLAN) according to the IEEE
802.11b/g standards and branded by an industry
group as Wi-Fi.

Another commonly discussed set of bands are
in the space between 5 GHz and 6 GHz where
the IEEE 802.11a standard is defined to operate.
The unlicensed allocations in this band have
been the subject of recent international harmo-

nization efforts through the ITU at the 2003 World Radiocommunication Conference (WRC-03). (For more information, see www.itu.int/ITU-R/conferences/wrc/wrc-03/index.asp.)

The Technology Lineup

802.11

The major standard body for defining unlicensed wireless communications schemes is the IEEE where these standards are part of the 802 series of standards. The best known of these wireless standards today is the 802.11 series which describe WLANs. These radio systems allow communications within a relatively small area, typically within about 100 meters of a central access point (AP).

A typical use of 802.11 today would be to place APs strategically around an office, each connected to the wired Internet, and thus allow any PCs or other data terminals in the area to get access to the network. These APs may be deployed privately and secured so that only, for example, employees of a business can use them, or they may be deployed publicly in a common place such as an airport or train station where any users may use them (either for free or for a service charge).

Any wireless data communications standard primarily consists of two layers. The first is a definition of a protocol that lets stations using the radio channel know when it is their turn to transmit and how actual data is packaged with information about who it is for and where it starts and stops in the signal. This layer is called the Media Access Control layer, or MAC. Below this layer is a definition of how an actual radio signal is modulated to encode information on it, which is called the physical layer, or PHY.

For 802.11, the MAC is optimized for a set of equally important systems as one typically finds on a local area network. A central AP manages the collection, giving each station that needs to send information a turn to do so. Since the AP may not always know that a remote system needs a slot, there are also periodic times when any station may transmit without permission. Because multiple stations may decide independently to do so at the same time, this sort of transmission is subject to collisions that require stations to waste time retransmitting their information. The combination of these managed and unmanaged periods, however, creates a stable system that allows all the network users to fairly share the limited capacity of the channel.

In the 802.11 family, the main standards are designated 802.11b, 802.11a, and 802.11g. These differ primarily in their definition of what PHY is used, though each expects to operate using about a 20-MHz wide channel. The first version to be deployed operated in the 2.4-GHz band and was designated 802.11b. The 802.11b standard defines operations at several different data rates, ranging from 1 Mbps up to 11 Mbps in each channel. How much data you can successfully transmit through a channel is primarily related to how strong the signal is compared with the background noise. This is similar to how well you can hear someone talking being a function of how loud they speak compared with how noisy the environment is. When the signal-to-noise ratio is good, you can achieve the higher data rates. Note that the farther away from a transmitter a receiver is located, the weaker the received signal will be. Thus poor signal-to-noise ratios can be the result of interference or simply that the source is distant.

The 802.11b PHY was designed to allow devices to efficiently share spectrum and to improve on earlier transmission schemes that had inferior performance in the presence of radio interferers (noise) and reflected signals (called multipath). The 802.11b PHY uses a scheme called Direct Sequence Spread Spectrum (DSSS) to transmit signals over the air. DSSS provides some protection against interferers such as the radiation from microwave ovens or 2.4-GHz cordless phones. 802.11b's lower data rates (1 Mbps and 2 Mbps) use a technique called Barker coding in conjunction with DSSS which can work in poor signal conditions; whereas 802.11b's higher data rates (5.5 Mbps and 11 Mbps) use an alternative technique called Complementary Code Keying (CCK) in conjunction with DSSS.

There are only a limited number of distinct 11b

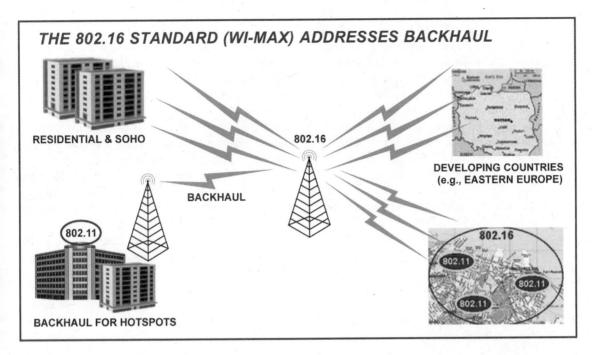

THE 802.16 STANDARD (WI-MAX) ADDRESSES BACKHAUL

RESIDENTIAL & SOHO

802.16

DEVELOPING COUNTRIES
(e.g., EASTERN EUROPE)

BACKHAUL

802.11

BACKHAUL FOR HOTSPOTS

802.16
802.11
802.11
802.11

channels available because typically this band is less than 100MHz wide and other radio allocations on either side mean that it isn't practical to expand the band internationally. To make available more WLAN capacity, regulators have agreed to allocations between 5 and 6 GHz. 802.11a is a version of the standard designed to operate in these bands, and it is now beginning to come on the market. This version of the standard also differs from the 802.11b standard by using more advanced PHY techniques that allow it to have a maximum data rate of 54 Mbps. A more recent standard called 802.11g applies similar advanced PHY techniques in the 2.4 GHz band to achieve operation up to 54 Mbps. Looking past 802.11a and 802.11g, work continues in the standards body to look at even more advanced PHY techniques to continually improve the robustness and speed of WLAN systems.

The 802.11 standards committee also defines other aspects of the standard in associated specification such as 802.11e which will describe quality-of-service enhancements and 802.11i which will improve security protocols.

As 802.11 systems have become increasingly

available and useful, we are now seeing 802.11 capabilities being built into more consumer devices. For example, all mobile PCs that use Intel® Centrino™ Mobile Technology come equipped to access the network using 802.11. We are also beginning to see PDAs and even phones that use 802.11 to communicate.

While 802.11 standards are designed technically for short-range operations, some users have created somewhat nonstandard equipment that is capable of longer-range operation of up to multiple kilometers. The required modifications include special antennas, boosted power output, and changes to detailed aspects of the data encoding to allow for the longer time taken by signals that need to travel such distances. A better and standardized solution to longer-range data communications can be found in a parallel standard that has recently been developed, IEEE 802.16.

802.16

As with 802.11, 802.16 is actually a family of standards, some completed and some still in progress. This family also has an associated industry group, WiMax. The original 802.16 standard defines a MAC suitable for an access system based at a central base station and serving multiple users scattered over a relatively large area whose radius can be many kilometers. This version of the standard also defines a particular physical layer (PHY) that is suited for use in bands between 10 and 66 GHz. The standard is optimized for providing an access service to, for example, an entire building where multiple systems within the building can all be attached to the single building transceiver.

It is helpful to think of 802.16 as an alternative to a wire or fiber for delivering an Internet connection to a site. Unlike 802.11, this standard does not narrowly define the frequency bands that should be used nor limit the channel width. It can therefore accommodate whatever bands, licensed or unlicensed, that may be available to an operator. For example, with a 20-MHz channel available and a strong signal between the base station and remote site, the capacity can be as high as 96 Mbps while a 28-MHz channel in a similar situation could achieve over 130-Mbps. On the other hand, remote sites at the fringe of reception of a base station might only be able to achieve a 32-Mbps capacity. Of course, as a multipoint system expected to serve many customers, these capacities must be shared across all the served users.

Another member of this standards family, 802.16a is optimized for operation in frequencies between 2 and 11 GHz. It is also yet more flexible in channel width choices, including channels as narrow as 1.75 MHz to allow it to be used where only small allocations are available. This version is attracting considerable commercial attention now because this range covers a number of attractive bands found around the world.

First, the unlicensed bands described earlier fall into this range. 802.16a systems are long-range systems and therefore at first look do not appear attractive for use in unlicensed bands where interference among competing operators could become a problem. However, particularly in rural and developing markets it is likely that there will be sufficient unlicensed spectrum and little enough competition for it that operators may find its use quite reasonable.

There are also commonly available bands at 2.5 GHz and 3.4 GHz in various countries that are licensable for use with an access data service. 802.16a looks to be a good choice for these systems as well. An operator licensed to have exclusive use of part of one of these bands could offer broadband wireless access in more densely populated urban or suburban areas without interference concerns.

One key issue for wireless access systems such as 802.16 is whether they require line-of-sight, or LOS, between the receiver and the base station or whether near LOS or non-LOS is sufficient. Ideally, LOS would not be required, but the reality is that radio waves are always attenuated when passing through obstacles so that non-LOS performance will always be poorer than LOS performance. For good performance, the best design will be an end station that mounts at least the antenna on the outside of the building facing generally in the direction of the base station. While possibly complicating installation slightly, this will assure the best range and performance for an 802.16 deployment.

3G and beyond

It is worth briefly relating these data communications standards with the evolution of conventional cellular telephony as it adds data communications services. 802.16 starts from the premise of delivering broadband data to fixed points. For example, it generally assumes a reasonable wide channel allocation. To this it is adding mobility capabilities via 802.16e, which will allow it to support at least a nomadic model; that is, one where an end station doesn't move much while operating but may move around between sessions. It has also been adding support for narrow channels. Higher degrees of mobility will also require considerably more support for handing active connections off between base stations. On this infrastructure, one can then think about running Voice-over Internet packets, or VoIP, to provide standard telephony service.

3G cellular systems start with the premise of delivering highly mobile voice services and increasing narrow- to mid-bandwidth data services. Their infrastructure is optimized for high mobility including high-speed handoff. Data services are carried over a somewhat more complex technical structure designed for these needs.

For the immediate future, what infrastructure to deploy will be determined by previous investments in infrastructure (e.g., an existing 2G cellular system) or the specific needs (e.g., good data services to remote rural areas with little mobility needs). Looking forward, 4G systems are at this point primarily just a name. A good working assumption, however, is that 4G systems will be a marriage of the best attributes of 3G cellular and packet-based wireless access systems.

There is still uncertainty about where such standards will be developed. Data standards have been defined to data mainly in IEEE while cellular standards have come from the ITU. A new group within the IEEE, 802.20, has begun to look at highly mobile systems from a data-centric view. At this point, it is too early to decide how 802.20, continued improvements to 802.16, and various possible 3G follow-on standards will relate to one another.

One other trend worth noting is toward end-user devices that can interact with multiple types of networks. Clearly, PCs are intelligent enough devices that they can easily support multiple radios or flexible radios that will permit them to communicate using multiple standards, choosing the best available network be it 802.11, 802.16, or a wide-area cellular technology such as GPRS. Smaller devices including PDAs and voice handsets will also evolve to support multiple networks. For example, a carrier may support a handset that uses Voice-over IP (VoIP) over 802.11 if it finds itself in a place where such a WLAN is present but switch to a standard cellular mode otherwise. Considerable technical work is still required to define the standards needed to make smooth transitions across such disparate networks work well.

System Architecture Issues

Wired versus wireless options

Any wireless access network eventually gets connected to the wired Internet, so it is important to understand the role of wireless with regard to wired parts of a deployment. Wireless systems have a number of advantages of which the two most notable are the portability of the end systems and the ability to deploy without extensive laying of physical wires or fibers. It is important to realize, however, that wireless systems pay for these advantages: They will never be as high performance as a fiber deployment. Consequently, it is best to see wireless systems as complementing rather than replacing wired ones.

Ideally, fiber would be deployed as deeply into a deployment as affordable and practical. Whenever new "wires" need to be deployed to carry data, fiber systems are clearly the right choice. Wireless would then be used to extend this connectivity to a larger number of locations and to ultimately connect end systems to the network. However, sensible deployments will utilize good copper connections that may already be in place to feed wireless systems, and wireless access systems may well feed locations such as offices that may have an internal wired Ethernet system in place. Thus, most real-world deployments will use both wired and wireless technologies in a cost-effective mix to reach the most users.

Mesh and multi-hop approaches

Up to this point, wireless systems have been discussed as consisting of base stations or access points (APs) that feed a collection of end systems. But more complex wireless systems make good sense as well. For example, a simple case would consist of an 802.16 wireless-access system with an antenna on the side of a building that is wired to an 802.11 AP inside the building with which end systems communicate.

A more complex example is a multi-hop 802.16 system. Rather than feeding an 802.16 base station directly with a fiber, one might feed it with a link from another 802.16 base station. Of course, careful channel selection is required so that the feeder signal from the first base station does not interfere with the distribution signal sent from the end base station, but such a system might avoid considerable construction of fiber links when serving

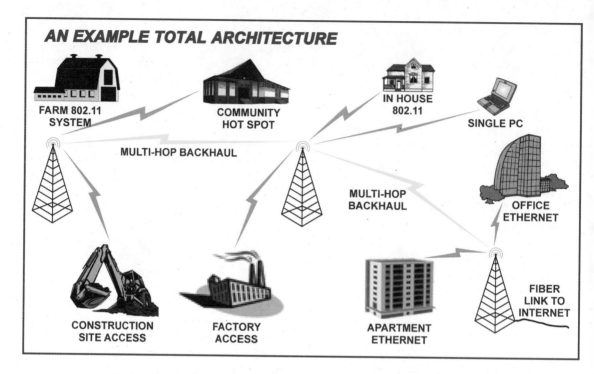

AN EXAMPLE TOTAL ARCHITECTURE

FARM 802.11 SYSTEM

COMMUNITY HOT SPOT

IN HOUSE 802.11

SINGLE PC

MULTI-HOP BACKHAUL

MULTI-HOP BACKHAUL

OFFICE ETHERNET

CONSTRUCTION SITE ACCESS

FACTORY ACCESS

APARTMENT ETHERNET

FIBER LINK TO INTERNET

sparsely populated areas. Technical considerations will limit the effectiveness of this approach. Increasing the number of hops will add to the network latency seen by the end systems which can eventually adversely impact some applications such as voice.

In designing multi-hop links that will carry latency sensitive traffic, one needs to define an acceptable latency budget and then compute the latency added for each relay point. Generally, a few hops can be tolerated without unacceptable degradation to voice traffic (i.e., latencies worse than what is experienced by cell users or general VoIP users today). The specific limits will depend on the specifications of the actual equipment, however. Another limiter to multi-hop deployments is that the traffic from outlying base stations will fan in eventually to a common link to the high-performance fiber backbone, and the total capacity of the common links can eventually limit total system performance.

An even more complex system architecture that may be appropriate for some deployments is a mesh network. Such designs are still in the research stage today but will likely be incorporated into future standards. In a mesh design all, or at least very many, end-point nodes also act as relay points to other end-point nodes. Essentially traffic to many users is carried through radios at their neighbors' homes. This reduces the number of explicit base stations that are needed by turning every end point into a sort of mini-base station. For cases where the end points to be served are very sparse, this may reduce deployment costs by eliminating central base stations in favor of adding small incremental costs to many user stations. For more dense deployments, mesh systems can increase reliability and capacity because there may be many traffic paths back to the Internet.

An example total architecture

We can summarize much of the discussion above by considering a figure (above) that illustrates many of the deployment options. Any real deployment may only use a subset of the cases illustrated, but all the cases will likely appear in some deployment.

The effective combination of 802.16, 802.11,

and fiber and wired infrastructure can support a wide variety of cost-effective Internet access ranging from traditional office access to remote agricultural and community systems supporting rural development. It is worth noting that while the mobility benefits of wireless access may be viewed as mainly of interest as a luxury for developed economies, they may be beneficial even in developing economies as a way to support such activities as development construction, outdoor industries such as farming, drilling, or mining, or even roving governmental services teams for things like medical outreach.

The Importance of Standards

Standards are discsussed at length above, and it is quite important to realize how important standards actually are. First, standards create a way for the best technical ideas from academic and industry developers to be combined and amplified. The process of creating the standard subjects the proposed ideas to broad review and generally results in considerable technical improvements on any individual company proposals.

Of great importance to purchasers of the ultimate equipment, standards generally result in much lower costs much sooner. This is because the existence of a standard creates a common market into which competing companies sell. Furthermore, the size of that common market is larger than any submarket based on proprietary approaches would be. In the high-technology world, costs are strongly a function of volumes so the creation of a single high-volume market leads to much lower costs than a fragmented market would. Standards also permit higher degrees of integration of equipment, which also contributes to lower costs.

For communications gear, particularly mobile equipment, standards are critical to allowing users to move around countries and the world while still having their equipment work correctly. While this may not seem to be of direct importance to the use of communications equipment to connect the citizens of developing countries, it will in fact enable those citizens to more easily become part of the world economy and benefit from the resulting development. For example, while mobility may not be important to providing access to the residents of a farm, it may be important to the visiting businesspeople who are negotiating for the exports of their crops or the introduction of new economic development projects to the area.

Future Directions

Radio technology and standards are still very much in a period of active and successful development. The performance of the technologies is still limited by the amount of cost-effective computing power that can be applied to the problem. The problem of reconstructing a data stream from a received encoded radio wave is one that is solved with complex signal processing mathematics. As processors get faster, more complex algorithms become cost effective and the performance of digital radio systems improves. While there are certainly theoretical limits to such improvements, today there is still quite a way to go to reach them, and therefore we should expect continued technology evolution.

For example, the 802.11 group has begun discussions regarding the next generation of the family of standards in a workgroup called 802.11n. While it is too early to know what the performance improvements will be, it is reasonable to expect that the group will target transmission speeds above 100 Mbps and/or improvements in the range over which transmissions at high speed can occur. In addition to continuing to increase the complexity of the PHY encoding schemes, there are also entirely new techniques becoming available, such as "smart antennas" that will use processing power to benefit application performance.

Radios that use the spectrum in different ways are also being considered. One example is a technique called Ultra Wideband, or UWB. In this approach, vast bands of spectrum are used at extremely low power to transmit information very fast but only over very short distances. The approach allows multiple uses of the same spectrum since this UWB signal is so weak that exist-

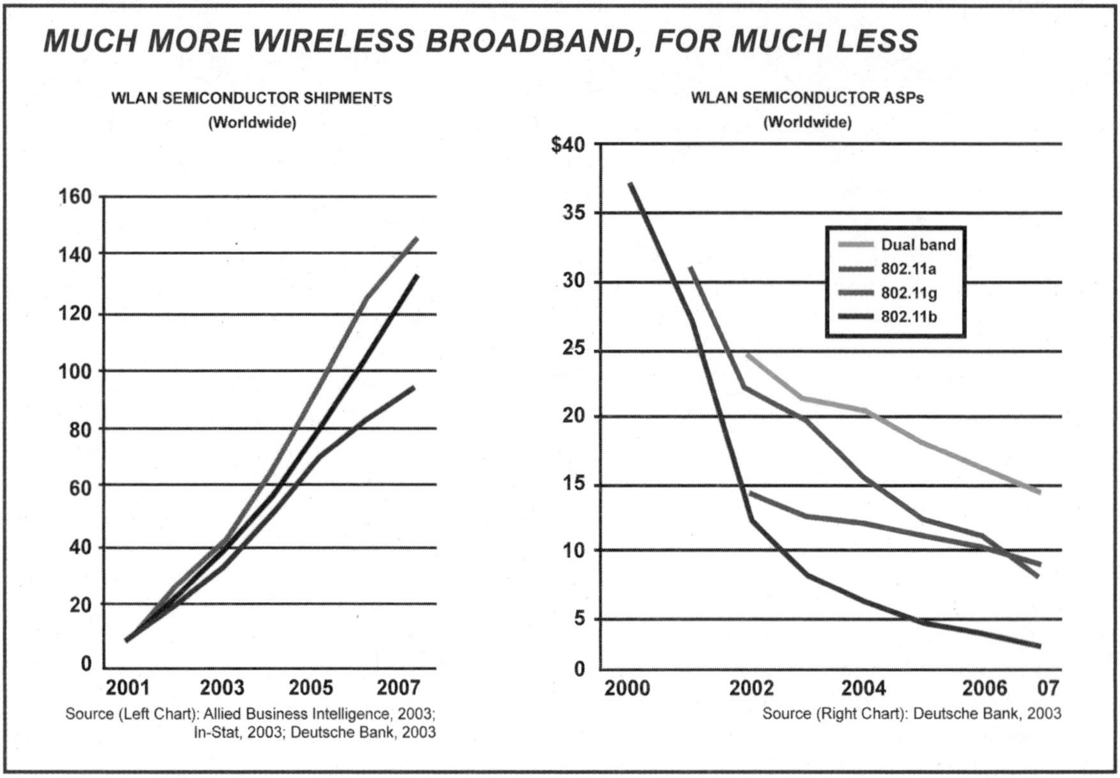
MUCH MORE WIRELESS BROADBAND, FOR MUCH LESS
WLAN SEMICONDUCTOR SHIPMENTS
(Worldwide)
160
140
120
100
80
60
40
20
0
2001
2003
2005
2007
Source (Left Chart): Allied Business Intelligence, 2003; In-Stat, 2003; Deutsche Bank, 2003
WLAN SEMICONDUCTOR ASPs
(Worldwide)
$40
35
30
25
20
15
10
5
0
Dual band
802.11a
802.11g
802.11b
2000
2002
2004
2006
07
Source (Right Chart): Deutsche Bank, 2003

ing users of the spectrum see it as a small amount of noise that can be ignored. In other schemes, smart or agile radios are being considered that can listen to spectrum bands to see if they are currently in use by their official owner, and if not, opportunistically use them to transmit data. Such radios could allow much more total efficiency in the use of spectrum than our more typical fixed allocations permit. Many of these new radio approaches, however, will require that regulators redesign their spectrum regulations to be more flexible. It will be critical for regulators to understand how they can accommodate such radically new approaches lest these radios be precluded from operating in their countries.

Closer to the application layers, there is also much work ongoing in providing better user experiences. For example, it will become possible to build phones that can seamlessly roam from 802.11 systems to 802.16 systems to cellular systems. This could permit a single handset to operate with a business as an extension but then behave as a cellular phone when its user departs the building.

About the only thing that is certain about the directions radio technology will take over the coming years is that it will become increasingly digital, increasingly "smart," and continue to change. The biggest impediment to the deployment of these new technologies may well be the inadvertent barriers created by old regulations that preclude deployment. The technology challenges will therefore be shared among the technologists, the regulators, and those who wish to deploy useful technologies. (Ⅱ)

REGULATORY ENVIRONMENT

A global standard meets local policies and politics*

By Axel Leblois

INTERNATIONAL INSTITUTIONS AND NATIONAL governments regularly publish announcements about the attribution of spectrum portions to certain applications and service providers. Beyond the simple sharing of a limited spectrum, however, the challenges facing wireless technology implementation in the developed and developing worlds involve many different actors. These include governments, regulatory agencies, local governments, and in many developing countries, incumbent telecom monopolies.

Incumbent Telecoms

While developed countries have started or completed deregulation of the communications markets, many emerging economies still run their telecom networks through a single, often state-owned organization. These monopolies are the de facto sole providers of technology, transmission, and content.

Over the years, these organizations have invested heavily in wire and cable communications infrastructure and are not yet ready to support wireless initiatives, much less to open the way to what may be perceived as potentially disruptive low-cost competition. This protective stance is often exacerbated by financial constraints because wire and cable infrastructure have been financed through debt. Quite often, incumbent telecoms also maintain tight control of national Internet backbone resources, making it difficult if not impossible for new wireless Internet service providers to operate.

The pressure exerted by such organizations to limit the access to new technology and service providers is, in some cases, encouraged by political restrictions on information access. In most cases, the result is a wireless market strewn with procedural hurdles that can prevent new actors from entering the field.

Unlicensed Spectrum

Only 41 percent of developing countries allow unlicensed use of wireless Internet devices and/or spectrum, compared with 96 percent of developed countries (see Table 1). Most newcomers to the telecommunications field in emerging economies face red tape and then a series of fees to obtain licenses for equipment and/or spectrum use. For example, countries charge license fees for hotspot equipment or sites and one-time or annual license fees for access-point devices.

Most researchers, analysts, and entrepreneurs see the need for a comprehensive regulatory framework for using limited spectrum. Presently, the unlicensed wireless spectrum was set around the 2.4-Ghz band. In June 2003, the International Telecommunications Union made available the 5-Ghz band for license-exempt technology deployment.

The 900-Mhz band, unlicensed in the United States, is presently used by the international GSM wireless phone standard, used in Western Europe and in many developing countries.

Axel Leblois is Co-Founder of the Wireless Internet Institute and President of World Times, Inc.

*Based on the proceedings of "The Wireless Internet Opportunity for Developing Countries" at UN Headquarters on June 26, 2003

	Developed countries	Developing countries
% with license-exempt wireless spectrum	96%	41%
% with license-exempt wireless devices	95%	40%
% with license-exempt wireless commerce	65%	20%

Source: UN BCS @ CeBit June 2003

Table 1: Licensing regulations for wireless Internet in developed and developing countries.

Within those internationally defined zones, national regulations vary widely, with more or less restrictions applying to radiation power. What is lacking is a comprehensive worldwide policy that would align countries and best practices among independent wireless Internet service providers around the world.

On March 20, 2003, in a positive step toward greater international consistency, the European Commission issued a recommendation to encourage member states to provide license-exempt WLAN access to public electronic communications networks and services in the available 2.4-Ghz and 5-Ghz bands. This is not binding on member states, but it is consistent with the (binding) Authorization Directive, which requires all member states to allow license-exempt access to the spectrum when the risk of harmful interference is negligible. The Authorization Directive was scheduled to be implemented by Member States on July 25, 2003.

The recommendation is important because it opens the way for using license-exempt spectrum for commercial purposes, creating large opportunities for service providers, and showing how fast changes have occurred given the amounts recently paid by mobile operators for access to the 3G spectrums. Here, access to the spectrum is free.

But it also introduces new issues, which operators of radio systems did not have to deal with in the past, in particular the obligation of noninterference already in place in the United States (see p. 20).

Unlicensed Doesn't Mean Unregulated

Many analysts emphasize that unlicensed does not mean unregulated, and all manner of operator providing wireless services still needs to maintain a no-interference working plan and a "good neighbor" attitude.

Conversely, licensing does not always promote the development of services. In the United States, for example, many licenses are attributed to providers that go no farther than the paper they are printed on! Several countries have early on embarked on various options for licensing, such as class licensing and service (as opposed to equipment) licensing. Many of those experiments are still under way, and they hold the promise of opening access to actors in underserved areas through a less cumbersome regulated environment.

Whatever solutions are chosen, enforcing an orderly use of the spectrum and an acceptable quality of the systems may require setting up unbiased oversight bodies with legal authority and a clear charter to promote the broadest access possible to users at the lowest possible cost.

ISPs Versus Network Providers

The provision of unlicensed wireless services raises further questions because of the two different kinds of actors in the field: network providers and Internet service providers. Of course, the two may be the same. When this is the case—that is, the ISP and network provider are affiliated—the two together will try to curb all competition. In countries where Internet service comes only from the incumbent telecom, competition is effectively curtailed, and a fair playing field is very hard to establish. Special interests will do everything in their power to hold on to their monopolies. This is particularly problematic when ISPs need to access the incumbent's network.

Consequently, both Internet-service entrepreneurs and end users can argue for unlicensing all together, letting markets drive both the choice of technology and the services offered. The rapid development of advanced wireless Internet technologies is compelling evidence of how robust markets quickly create a fair playing field. Both incumbents and newcomers must then adjust to the needs of the market, complementing one another rather than strictly competing.

Forward Agenda for Regulators

With both the North American and European markets taking ever more advantage of wireless Internet technologies using unlicensed spectrum, it seems ineluctable that wireless Internet solutions will gather great momentum and further benefit from economies of scale. Developing countries have the opportunity to assess when and how to transition toward similar unlicensed-spectrum definitions.

To draft a forward agenda, both government agencies and the private sector should make a thorough analysis of market potentials and the technologies that best suit a particular setting. A strong push for dissemination of knowledge in the sector seems indispensable. Internet access in general, and wireless Internet possibilities in particular, are seldom at the top of the agendas of government agencies. A comprehensive catalogue of potential applications, especially in e-education and e-health, is needed to expand policymakers' awareness.

The same goes for available technology, which remains in the somewhat guarded realm of technology wizards. Regulatory bodies need to be

Voice-over IP in potentia

Although the issue of voice-over IP is not specific to the wireless Internet, it deserves special attention. The development of voice-over IP has been extremely rapid in most developing countries, driven by international traffic bypassing traditional circuit-switched accounting and international settlements. Consequently, many telecoms have been initially concerned about related losses of revenues, especially where international calls subsidize local traffic. This explains the very strong opposition to voice-over IP expressed at multiple occasions by certain developing countries.

At the same time, others have concluded that voice-over IP could yield significant savings in hard currency if national telecoms use the services of international voice-over IP operators. This strategy would eliminate the settlement rate balancing tariffs, saving around 50 percent of the cost of terminating international calls.

Voice-over IP technology has been adopted by several developing-country telecoms to build more efficient (lower bandwidth required), lower-cost networks. Examples include Chad, Egypt, Venezuela, South Africa, and Nigeria, with many more in transition. Countries are taking a further step by allowing the licensing of IP telephony providers. An example is India, whose regulations once prohibited most commercial forms of voice-over IP to protect its telecommunications industry. The net result of these trends is a likely rapid expansion of voice-over IP in developing countries both from an international traffic and domestic network standpoint.

Although the debate on voice-over IP in the context of wireless Internet has not yet emerged, it seems that well-designed local regulatory frameworks supporting the deployment of voice-over IP by local wireless Internet service providers could potentially accelerate both the availability of telephony in underserved areas and vastly improve the economics of wireless Internet by adding voice to data traffic. ◑

—*Axel Leblois*

enlightened on the options for distance and proximity transmission equipments, and on the technical knowledge necessary for implementation and maintenance. This is particularly true in remote underserved areas where the expertise to sustain a working system may be unavailable. Technical education programs should be delivered by providers on an ongoing basis, in cooperation with international institutions and regulatory bodies.

Last but not least, guidelines are needed to help assess the economic sustainability of wireless Internet access systems. Today's last-mile solutions can bring access to the most underserved and poor areas. The financing of such networks in itself does not constitute a major obstacle to implementation, but the financial aspects of content sale and use are still pretty much undefined. The legal and economic framework for existing providers and newcomers to develop those systems should comprised of incentives for sustainable and financially sound programs.

A competitive regulatory environment, free access to spectrum within guidelines, alliances between private sector and government bodies, and between incumbent telecommunications providers and newcomers, and an international agreement on the basic framework available to wireless Internet systems can nurture the development of the networks and further bridge the digital divide. Multi-partner discussions are strongly encouraged, lest the market take the lead. ◍

FCC regulates the technology

In the United States, regulation of the wireless Internet now focuses primarily on technology standards. If manufacturers, practitioners, and entrepreneurs adhere to technical standards designed to deal with interference, no approvals are required to operate equipment. You can buy it, take it out of the box, turn it on, and use it. At the same time, because operators have no vested rights to continue operation, this constitutes a nonexclusive use of the radio spectrum.

At "The Wireless Internet Opportunity for Developing Countries" conference at UN Headquarters on June 26, 2003, Robert Pepper, Chief of the Office of Plans and Policy at the FCC, touched on the dynamics of unlicensed spectrum, technology regulation, and markets.

"Because of the newer technologies, you can do a lot with unlicensed spectrum. Under our rules, you may not cause harmful interference. And you must accept interference from somebody else. As a result, the technology companies are continuing to develop increasingly robust technologies that are smart enough to know when there's someone else in the neighborhood, in order to avoid interference from someone else that you might be receiving.

"You must stop your operation if notified by the FCC that your device is causing harmful interference. From a regulator's perspective, it's not only important to establish the baseline rules for the technology, but you also need—and this is important around the world—to be able to detect people who are violating those technical rules, and have the ability to enforce those rules so you can put them out of business. None of this works unless people adhere to these rules, and then they can operate on an unlicensed basis—easy entry, easy exit—using declining-cost technology based on global standards.

"You also must receive authorization before marketing or importing these devices into the United States. This all goes to the notion of regulating a device, and not regulating spectrum or use of spectrum. We permit very flexible use of that spectrum as long as your devices adhere

▶

Microsoft chief reports on WRC-03

THE 2003 WORLD RADIO-COMMUNICATION Conference finished its nearly month-long session in Geneva, Switzerland, on July 4, and took an enormous step forward in promoting unlicensed wireless broadband data services.

At the WRC-03, delegates harmonized preexisting, regional allocations of unlicensed spectrum in the 5-Ghz band, creating a greatly expanded, global allocation of 455-Mhz of spectrum for use by unlicensed wireless networking devices. This decision should significantly broaden the opportunities for people to access information using unlicensed devices, such as Wi-Fi wireless LANs. It is also likely to enable faster deployment of wireless data services in locations where dial-up access is not practical.

The WRC's recent vote was the culmination of a cooperative effort between US government officials and more than 2,500 delegates from countries around the world. Representatives from companies such as Microsoft, Intel, Hewlett-Packard, and Cisco worked very closely with US officials in the months leading up to the WRC to create a framework for spectrum allocation that met the concerns of incumbent users, reflected global considerations, and enabled a global market for unlicensed broadband equipment.

In the case of the radio spectrum and the United States, Microsoft and its technology-industry partners will support the FCC as it codifies the WRC decisions and allocates the US radio spectrum. As this process is mirrored around the world, it will help make possible consistent availability of unlicensed radio spectrum that will enable people worldwide to access the Internet and to communicate locally and globally.

Pierre De Vries, Chief of Technology Incubation for Microsoft, predicts the WRC decision will accelerate Wi-Fi as a new broadband platform in homes, businesses, and schools in developing as well as in developed nations, resulting in "a rapid deployment of innovative wireless data and services for business, personal and educational applications."

Q. Do you expect this decision to benefit developing countries as well?

A. Certainly. Unlicensed wireless technology can help developing countries implement Internet networks very quickly, and that has significant implications for accelerating the growth of information systems in those nations. We are also seeing rural and suburban applications in developed nations taking advantage of Wi-Fi. Wi-Fi is a technology with broad potential around the world, and we think the WRC agreement underscores that.

Q. Why did the US government and technology companies come together on this issue?

A. Everybody had a clear sense from the start that allocating spectrum to unlicensed wireless connectivity would have a very positive impact on accelerating the delivery of broadband networks and data worldwide. This was a goal that both government bodies and the private sector felt was worth achieving, and one that we all worked together on.

Q. Is the WRC decision binding?

A. Yes, in the sense that any spectrum used consistent with this new primary allocation receives worldwide interference protection. And equally important, the WRC decision is a strong signal to governments globally that they should implement this decision on a national level. We believe that most of them will.

Q. In the developing world, isn't the cost of devices and wireless data services still a consideration?

A. It certainly is, but no one is saying this will result in millions of Web-enabled devices being deployed in the developing world overnight. But by allocating spectrum in this fashion, the WRC has given governments and the technology industry a clear path to growing communication, connectivity, and commerce around the globe. Having everyone moving along a common path is a major step forward.

Q. What was the role of Microsoft, H-P, Intel, and Cisco in the WRC decision?

A. We all worked very closely with government officials and WRC attendees. This was clearly a case where the industry as a whole benefited from a broad policy decision, and where everyone concerned realized that there was a greater benefit that could be delivered by working cooperatively on this.

Q. What are the next steps in this process?

A. Each government that participated in the WRC will now go back and work through its regulatory agencies to codify the decisions made there. This particular decision was one of many decisions, so all of the delegates will have lots of ground to cover with their respective agencies. We're ready to work with the other industry leaders and with the FCC to make the WRC decision a reality for the United States.

Q. Will Microsoft be working with government bodies in countries other than the United States, as well as with the FCC?

A. Each government must deal with the issue independently. We believe the WRC decision speaks volumes about the need for a worldwide capability for unlicensed spectrum, and we believe that all the various international regulatory bodies will feel the same way. It truly is a win-win on a worldwide basis for service providers, hardware and software companies, and most importantly, for customers. ◖

▶

to the rules....

"It's hard to predict the future, but we know it's already happened. We're looking at millions of uses with wireless. The wireless networks in the United States are expected to top 15,000 by the end of this year. That's up by a factor of 15 from two years ago. And it's not just wireless local area network. We also see various versions and flavors of Wi-Fi including 802.16 as wireless local loop.

"These technologies are enabling new services in the developing world. In the United States, we also have our own version of the developing world: very rural areas. We have seen Wi-Fi technologies being deployed in our rural areas with stations on water towers and grain elevators, providing broadband services to farmers. There are some very low-density areas that could never get it before, through little companies that are breaking even with 400 customers. It's very exciting and it totally changes the business model. This is why we think this a very important technology for the developing world globally." ◖

OPPORTUNITIES AND ROADBLOCKS

Toward a broadband village area network

By Sandy Pentland

THE GOAL FOR THE INFORMATION SOCIETY should be broadband connectivity every-where, rather than the village telephone envisioned in many current programs. While this may seem unrealistic, recent advances in technology make it an achievable goal, especially when adopted as part of a progressive, market-driven migration from government seed services, such as e-governance, to universal broadband connectivity paid for by local users.

The key change is that recent advances in wireless computer networking—particularly the IEEE 802.xx standards—have led to huge commercial success and very low pricing for broadband networks. While these networks are thought of as mainly for offices, we have shown that they can provide broadband access to even the most remote areas at very low prices. Today wireless cell-phone and wireless local-loop, or WLL, service costs about one third of copper or fiber land-line service, while packet-based broadband computer networks cost roughly one ninth of the land-line service-and have the additional advantage of being far friendlier to data services, and to lower-grade voice service such as voice messaging. These new technologies offer developing countries an opportunity to leapfrog over wireline and wireless-local-loop telephony infrastructure to the forefront of broadband communications technology.

Wireless data networks based on the IEEE 802.11 or so-called Wi-Fi standard are perhaps the most promising wireless technology. The forces driving the standardization and proliferation of Wi-Fi in the developed world have resulted in features that can stimulate the communications market in the developing world. These features include: its ease of set-up, use, and maintenance; its relatively high bandwidth; and, most importantly, its relatively low cost for both users and providers.

Standard Wi-Fi connectivity (the IEEE 802.11b wireless standard) provides up to 11 Mbps data rates and operates in a band near 2.4 Ghz that is generally unlicensed in Europe and the Americas. Newer versions of Wi-Fi provide 22 Mbps in this band, and versions that operate at higher frequencies provide up to 54 Mbps. Tests in rural settings show that a standard Wi-Fi card (as commonly used with laptop PCs) can provide good connectivity up to a half-kilometer radius given line-of-sight. With the addition of antennas and repeaters, it is possible to achieve point-to-point connectivity at distances of up to 20 kilometers. Wi-Fi access points (devices commonly used to provide a Wi-Fi network) currently can be purchased for $80 and Wi-Fi cards for under $30.

As one demonstration of the practicality of this new technology for rural connectivity, researchers from the Indian Institute of Technology at Kanpur, working with Media Lab Asia, have "unwired" a 100-sq-km area of the Gangetic Plain in central India. This project provides broadband connectivity to the homes of almost one million people at under $40 per home. Other experiments have shown the practicality of the technology in mountainous terrain, and in city centers. Indeed, several cities in the United States have begun to deploy free Internet connectivity using the IEEE 802.11b wireless standard.

Even with advances such as demonstrated in the Digital Gangetic Plain project, the cost of real-time,

Professor Alex (Sandy) Pentland is Director of Media Lab Asia, Co-Director of the Digital Nations Consortium, and Toshiba Professor at the MIT Media Laboratory.

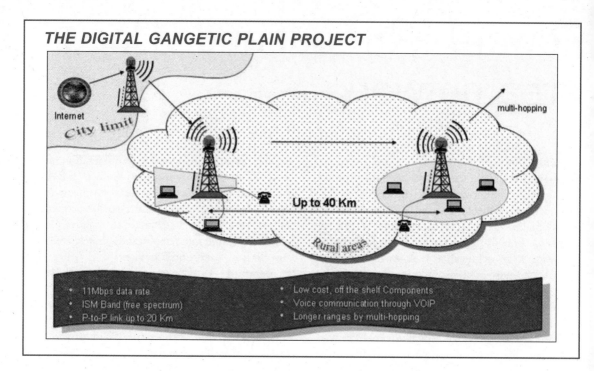

THE DIGITAL GANGETIC PLAIN PROJECT

Internet

City limit

multi-hopping

Up to 40 Km

Rural areas

- 11Mbps data rate
- ISM Band (free spectrum)
- P-to-P link up to 20 Km
- Low cost, off the shelf Components
- Voice communication through VOIP
- Longer ranges by multi-hopping

circuit-switched communications is sufficiently high that it may not be the appropriate starting point for rural connectivity. Based on market data for information and communication technology (ICT) services in rural India, it has been argued that asynchronous service—for example, voice messaging and e-mail—may be a more cost-effective starting point for rural-connectivity projects.

MIT Media Lab researchers have developed and demonstrated a combination of wireless technology and asynchronous delivery that reduces the cost of asynchronous Internet service by two orders of magnitude below land-line expenses. This store-and-forward wireless network for rural connectivity is known as DakNet (see p. 79).

The opportunity posed by these technical advances and field demonstrations is to redirect existing universal-service programs away from the copper-to-village-center model and toward a broadband village-area network serving everyone within the village center. Whether beginning with the inexpensive asynchronous service or the somewhat more expensive real-time service, such village-area communications can be smoothly upgraded to always-on universal broadband as market demand grows.

To achieve this goal, policy makers should be considering several policy steps.

The first step is to deregulate the portions of the radio spectrum used by the IEEE 802.xx standards. This spectrum is already deregulated in developed countries, which has unleashed an enormous commercial expansion and brought plummeting prices.

A second step is to permit voice-over Internet packets, or VoIP. Currently many countries strictly limit the carriers of real-time voice signal, but now that voice can be broken into Internet packets, or IP, these regulations are increasingly archaic and expensive and limit the growth of digital businesses.

Finally, regulators should consider deregulating mini Internet service providers, or ISPs. These are typically Internet-connected computer users, such as Internet cafés, that allow nearby users to access their Internet connection with an 802.11 wireless local area network. By allowing such connections, the evidence is that there will follow an explosion of connectivity within village and city centers. ◑

For the poor, connectivity means economic opportunity

By Iqbal Z. Quadir

INFORMATION AND COMMUNICATION TECHNOLO-gies have some good news for developing countries. These technologies can foster much-needed broad-based economic development, empowering people with possibilities that were once unthinkable. For instance, there are already more mobiles than fixed phones in Africa and, in the next five years, mobiles are expected to outnumber fixed phones 4 to 1. This rapid expansion of connectivity in Africa is surely more attributable to the new uses and economics of digital technologies than to anything else.

I can relate to this from my own experience in Bangladesh, where mobiles already outnumber fixed phones 2 to 1 and more and more people are able to coordinate their economic activities more effectively. They waste less time connecting with others and spend more time working together.

I first learned how connectivity can mean greater productivity about a decade ago, when I was working in a small investment firm in New York City. It was clear that our productivity had gone up after we adopted a rather rudimentary computer network. We began to avoid the cumbersome exchange of floppy disks, and we updated each other more frequently as our ideas evolved.

But one day this network broke down, and as I was waiting for someone to come fix it, I recalled a day from my childhood, in 1971, when Bangladesh was at war. My family had left the small town where we lived and moved to a relatively more peaceful rural area. One time my mother asked me to get some medicine for a sibling from someone about eight miles away. I walked all morning to get there, but when I arrived the medicine man wasn't there, and I spent all afternoon walking back home. Sitting in New York, I put the two experiences together and drew this conclusion: Whether you're in a modern office or in an underdeveloped village, connectivity is productivity.

To me, this meant that ordinary people could be economically empowered through telephones, and that telephones could become weapons against poverty. Connectivity allows people to better coordinate their activities and depend on one another more effectively. This dependability allows them to specialize in order to increase their productivity, which can allow them to pay for telephone service. If part of the increased productivity could be channeled to pay for the service, a viable commercial project could be constructed without too much concern about existing purchasing power.

Even though telephones are proven production tools and the increased productivity that results from using them outweighs the cost of installing them, virtually all poor countries have a shortage of telephones, even after a dramatic rise in the number of mobiles. The percentage of households who can afford a telephone tends to be much larger than the percentage that actually have one. In Bangladesh, in 1993, there were only two telephones per one thousand people, and almost all these phones were confined to a few urban pockets. In its rural areas, where 100 million people lived, there were virtually no telephones.

This led me to establish Gonofone Development Corp. in New York in 1994 with angel funding. The investors in Gonofone, which means "People's Phone," provided the seed funding to help me develop and organize what is now GrameenPhone, currently the

Iqbal Z. Quadir is a Lecturer at Harvard's Kennedy School of Government and Founder of GrameenPhone in Bangladesh.

largest telephone company in Bangladesh in terms of number of subscribers.

I realized that a large-scale commercial project that could serve all urban areas and 68,000 villages in Bangladesh would require players not only with large resources but the ability to make specific meaningful contributions in solving the problems on the ground, establishing a real telephone company and distributing the services in rural areas effectively. After studying the conditions in Bangladesh, I realized that a practical and dependable way of distributing the service in rural areas with little modern infrastructure was the key to a realistic and sustainable project.

To solve this practical problem, I felt that a micro-credit program made sense. For instance, small entrepreneurs, backed by micro-credit from Grameen Bank, could retail telephone services to their surrounding communities. Because Grameen Bank already had a branch network throughout the rural areas in Bangladesh and its repayment records were excellent, the Grameen borrower network would be an excellent way to penetrate the rural market. This practical scheme not only convinced Grameen Bank to join in the project but also attracted Telenor AS, the primary telephone company in Norway. Eventually, a global consortium emerged that additionally involved Marubeni Corp. in Japan; Asian Development Bank in the Philippines; Commonwealth Development Corp. in the United Kingdom; and

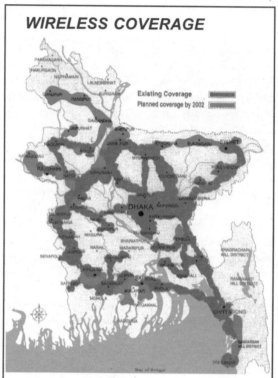

WIRELESS COVERAGE

Existing Coverage
Planned coverage by 2002

GrameenPhone serves 35,000 villages in rural Bangladesh.

International Finance Corp. and Gonofone in the United States. With the support of these investors, GrameenPhone, established in late 1996, started building a new cellular network and providing services to the public soon thereafter.

To date, GrameenPhone has built the largest cellular network in the country with investments exceeding $300 million and a subscriber base of more than a million. Its rural program is already available in more than 35,000 villages, providing telephone access to more than 50 million people, while helping to create micro-entrepreneurs in these villages. GrameenPhone is an example of technology dramatically unleashing new possibilities and, through specific projects, increasing broad-based empowerment.

Some people think that poor people are targets for aid, forgetting that people are the most important resource poor countries have. Development is not resource transfer from rich countries to poor ones but engagement of citizens in economically meaningful ways. In GraameenPhone, citizens are not just receiving a service, they are actively engaged in producing it.

While some people are worried about the purchasing power of citizens in poor countries for a service they may want to provide, citizens' involvement in distributing the service actually lowers costs and helps bring the service within the purchasing power. Moreover, the availability of a service makes people more productive and raises their purchasing power.

Others think that education is a project separate from economic activities. But engaging citizens in economic activities is an education in itself. One of the surprising aspects of the GrameenPhone experience is that the women who are selling the services generally need no more than two days, and usually one day, to be trained to operate mobile phones. Engaging in an economic activity is an education itself, and poor people, being more economically needy, are better learners when it comes to education that also enhances their incomes.

GrameenPhone proves that the possibilities opened up by new technologies and proper design can make universal access realistic, even amid poverty and other difficulties. Technologies like Wi-Fi, or 802.11, among others, are adding yet more possibilities and moving the technological capabilities to the point that technology no longer remains an issue. Virtually unlimited possibilities are becoming realistic. The real issues are the utility of the service, the delivery mechanism, and their economics. And here, GrameenPhone may indeed have something to teach, through the emphasis on delivery and the involvement of people.

GrameenPhone did not invent any technology. It simply found a new way of deploying a service rapidly and effectively and in an economically sound way, while engaging and consequently empowering poor people. Entrepreneurs and innovators need to focus on the delivery mechanism and how to engage people, with the likelihood that the right way to engage people may also lead to the right delivery mechanism.

There are, of course, challenges. The upfront costs of connectivity technology can still be high for a poor country. For example, GrameenPhone's initial outside capital was $120 million, and it took five years to assemble that capital. The bureaucracies in the regulatory bodies also pose a significant challenge. These things require involvement of large players. That is why, for example, shareholders and lenders in GrameenPhone tend to be large. But actual development happens when smaller entrepreneurs are activated. The smaller in size and the larger in number, the better they are for development. Third, poor infrastructure ecology poses yet another challenge. In a poor country, other services, whose quality determine the ease of introducing a new service, tend to be relatively poor.

These challenges are far less daunting in the context of Wi-Fi. First, you don't need big up-front costs. One installation can be made with a few thousand dollars and it can make the next installation easier. The low up-front costs can help the emergence of many small entrepreneurs, who contribute to genuine economic development, not only by spreading the economic benefits but also by dispersing power and helping democracy take root. The spectrum necessary for Wi-Fi requiring no license further makes it easier for small entrepreneurs to enter the business and pass on the savings to consumers.

Wi-Fi usually requires few up-front regulatory permissions and can eventually lead to regulations that are sensitive to the needs of consumers and providers. Except in very authoritarian countries of the developing world, Internet service providers, or ISPs, emerged in an unregulated environment. That is, in developing countries where regulations generally evolve very slowly, the Internet arrived relatively suddenly because developing countries' governments simply weren't prepared to regulate it. When the regulations did come, the government needed to be sensitive to the needs of the entrepreneurs and of the consumers who were already enjoying the service.

In the case of Wi-Fi, or in general for a technology where many entrepreneurs can emerge because of the economics of the technology, eventual regulations tend to be healthy. Entrepreneurs participating in the field can argue for their rights, making eventual regulations conducive to growth. The relative ease with which entrepreneurs can enter the business preserves competition and protects consumers, even without regulations. ◐

Wireless Internet ventures in developing countries

By Theodore H. Schell

THE EXAMPLES OF WIRELESS INTERNET SERVICE providers, or WISPs, in the Case Study Compendium are all works in progress. Each embodies the hope for economic success as well as an opportunity to contribute to the social and economic development of a country or region. Each shows the potential of wireless technology as an alternative to the traditional copper and fiber infrastructures that are the dominant means of providing access to basic voice and advanced data services.

But the successful exploitation of this new technology is not guaranteed, and multiple roadblocks can present themselves in virtually every context. The question is how can wireless Internet entrepreneurs and interested governmental and nongovernmental organizations identify the nontechnology core issues that may arise in order to develop well-grounded strategies to improve success?

The Business Opportunity Defined

All ventures begin by identifying an opportunity through a business plan. For wireless or other telecommunications infrastructure ventures in developing countries and underserved communities, the investment thesis typically runs along the following lines:

▶ Wi-Fi and other wireless technologies are inexpensive, within certain performance parameters, relative

Theodore H. Schell is the Founder of Cometa Networks. He is a former Senior Vice President for Strategy and Corporate Development at Sprint and has been a General Partner at Apax Partners. He served in the Carter Administration from 1978 to 1981.

to the cost of building virtually any alternative access plant. Consequently, they enable development of service offerings that hitherto would not exhibit the requisite price/performance characteristics.

▶ The operating costs of a wireless-based venture can also be considerably less expensive if contextually appropriate performance levels for reliability, customer service, and support are established; and if one manages the business to minimize demands on back-office billing and other support systems. This, coupled with the lower cost environment targeted for service, yields operating costs not only far below those in developed nations or advanced metropolitan areas, but also appropriate for the targeted market.

▶ Sufficient revenues can be generated to yield a positive cash flow. This is typically based on the view that in underserved areas, in both developing and advanced nations, a sufficient latent or unmet demand for the services exists among those with sufficient disposable income to pay the bill, that the balance of revenue and costs will assure a profit.

▶ The benefits are assumed to be sufficiently substantial from a political and social perspective, such that the government in general and the regulator in particular are assumed friendly and thus the cooperation of the dominant carrier(s) is also assumed; for example, interconnection costs are favorable, provisioning will be done in a rapid and efficient manner, outages will be expeditiously addressed. In addition, three additional and key assumptions are typically made:

▶ the target is outside the sphere of interest of the incumbent carriers, either too small or remote to command their attention given capital constraints and more compelling opportunities;

▶ aggressive pricing by the incumbent will not materialize in response to the challenger as it would devalue the existing revenue base of the incumbent, and thus the entrepreneur will be able to extract a fair margin; and

▶ should anti-competitive behavior come to pass, the regulator, in support of competition and of the social and economic benefits engendered, will act to assure that predatory or otherwise anti-competitive practices are stopped and the incumbent penalized severely.

Key Issues in Realizing the Opportunity

If all proves out, everybody wins. Seldom, however, has such happened. Consequently, in today's environment, still reeling from the meltdown of the global telecommunications industry of the past several years, and skeptical of the overall global economy, let alone that in developing countries or depressed regions, private investment capital will be extremely difficult to secure. Assuming projected costs stand up under close scrutiny, the key issues of the prospective investor will be the following, because each has occurred a sufficient number of times in both developing and developed countries to give pause to even the most risk-tolerant investor. The central questions are:

▶ Will sufficient demand in fact manifest itself?

▶ Can one really be assured that the dominant or monopoly incumbent carrier will not retaliate, and that the regulator will establish and aggressively enforce a competitive framework?

▶ Is there a real opportunity for financial liquidity; that is, will the business grow sufficiently large and profitable to attract a buyer or to enable it to become a public company so that the investors can realize and repatriate the value that has been created?

Space allows only a cursory characterization of each of these topics—sufficient to sensitize one to the issue.

Demand

Several factors underlie skepticism about the absolute level of demand likely to manifest itself.

First, 802.11 technology, the primary technology capturing the imagination of the entrepreneur, requires that the end user have access to 802.11 capable devices. Consequently,

demand for the service will be held hostage not simply to the marketing of the service but also to the diffusion of 802.11-enabled devices into the hands of the potential user, such as 802.11-enabled computers and phones. This cost must be accounted for.

In developed economies, 802.11 technology is only beginning to find its way into the mass market, though the abundance of computers, PDA's, and cell phones is such that if one simply assumes the market rate of customer-premises-equipment, or CPE, replenishment, not to mention new devices, tens of millions of Wi-Fi-enabled devices will diffuse into the market assuring a sufficient addressable market. As such, the question in advanced economies is simply one of price and utility. In developing markets, however, it is otherwise. Publicly available kiosks and computing centers will have to be established, initial computer purchases will have to occur as will upgrades of existing devices in order that individuals and businesses have the technological capability to enjoy the benefits of the low cost telecommunications infrastructure.

Second, while the cost of implementing the service may well be substantially lower, the environments in which it is being implemented—the target market—is typically smaller in absolute terms, particularly in developing countries, and typically has substantially less disposable income available. In all markets, the question of the sufficiency of scale to assure profitability will always loom, and prices will need to be set to reflect this. Consequently, the question is whether the revenue/cost equation is in fact solved in these markets.

Clearly, the calculus is much more optimistic than in the past, but the lingering question is whether or not, or in which places, there is a sufficient number of businesses and individuals with the disposable income to pay the bills, with or without public subsidy. It is clear that advanced telecommunications infrastructure is a *sine qua non* of economic development; but independent of development, there is insufficient resource to support the infrastructure without subsidy. While Wi-Fi improves the calculus, the key question is whether or not it is sufficient.

Competitive and regulatory response

The competitive and regulatory response to the entrepreneurial venture, even when it is created at the apparent behest of the regulator or government, is the most troublesome issue. Personally, I have encountered it in four developing countries. In each case, in spite of an encouraging regulator and a legislated framework for competition, and in spite of an incumbent who was either "uninterested" in the geography being addressed or, alternatively, faced a combination of incentives and penalties structured to assure "cooperation" with the emerging carrier, the new company suffered major retaliatory actions that were rationalized or ignored by the regulators.

Examples included the following: increased investment and predatory pricing occurred in a region where the incumbent was chastised by the regulator and in which it pledged not to invest further; interconnection rates were set untenably high with the concurrence of the regulator and in one instance, interconnection was denied for nearly two years; provisioning orders were routinely ignored leaving substantial areas unable to be served for considerable periods of time; billing support, required during transitional periods while data bases were being prepared for transfer, was inadequate, and the data base transfer delayed; and the list goes on. In a simple, Internet-only application, only a subset of such issues will apply, but nonetheless they remain substantial concerns.

It is in the very DNA of an incumbent to protect his franchise and to assure that a new challenger will not arise, even if the initial activities occur far from the major urban and commercial centers. And a start-up, with a lower-cost basis, building a business even in a territory of little interest to the incumbent, is tomorrow's competitor and therefore an incipient "enemy." How do they cause trouble? Interconnection with the existing network is slow-rolled, circuits are provisioned on a hit or miss basis, outages are repaired, but slowly; quality is not enforced on the leased lines; wholesale prices are set untenably high; and retail prices

are set to preclude the new service provider from earning an acceptable margin. Few and far between are the entrepreneurial ventures that do not have to turn to the incumbent for essential services; and when one does so, it puts the new venture at risk.

This issue has arisen in virtually every advanced economy seeking to interject competition into its communications market; and it will arise, in all probability, in every developing country, often exacerbated because the clearest way to profitability for the new venture is to market to the incumbent's most lucrative buyers, and he eventually turns to this market to hasten revenue growth.

The responsibility to assure the entrepreneur's opportunity falls to the regulator. A competitive framework must be put in place that ensures fair and competitive pricing and provisioning of services from the incumbent to the new service provider, and fair means prices set such that the new entrant can earn a profit. The regulations must be rigorously enforced, for if there is not a steep price to pay, the rules will be violated.

Ensuring competition is not an easy task. Incumbent telecommunications providers in developing countries are typically intimately related to the government if not a part of it. They have political acumen, bureaucratic savvy, and political and bureaucratic access. In the name of assuring their ability to perform and earn the required foreign payments and capital returns, they may well argue against increased competition; in the context of open markets, in spite of regulations to the contrary, they may act to assure their own survival, justifying actions after the fact in a politically palatable way. This is not cynicism, it happens. And just as the entrepreneur must be realistic that such may be faced even in the context of utilizing free, unlicensed spectrum; the government must step up to this challenge if the benefits of entrepreneurial activity based upon Wi-Fi technology are to be seized and maximized. It is difficult to count the amount of money that has been lost because the well-intended promise has not been kept.

Financial liquidity

Building a good business is, paradoxically, not a

sufficient condition to attract many investors. Often, the question comes down to two additional issues. Will the business become large enough to attract a buyer; or to enable a public offering, assuming the existence of an appropriate market? Does the political environment enable the repatriation of dividends and/or capital gains? Both conditions are requisite to attract most sources of private investment capital.

Conclusion

Market savvy will develop, business plans will be refined, and many practical, day-to-day operating issues will be overcome. Wireless technology will assuredly advance, its costs will come down still further; and, it will be joined by an array of other technologies that will facilitate implementation of compelling hybrid, cost-effective networks. But two factors emphasized above are outside the control of the entrepreneur and the technology suppliers, and their appropriate resolution cannot be taken for granted. They merit repetition.

First, a competitive framework permissive of exploitation of new technologies and unlicensed spectrum by new, entrepreneurial organizations is a prerequisite; it cannot be compromised. The governmental regulators must establish it and enforce both its letter and its spirit, or entrepreneurial promise will whither and die.

Second, nontraditional financing must be made available in many markets, for until such time as the robustness of these fledgling enterprises can be convincingly demonstrated, they are likely to be capital starved. Will there be exceptions? Yes, and there are case studies in this volume that speak to them. But these are exceptions typically in rapidly advancing economies. Enabling the development of these ventures in some of the neediest locales will fall to governments, NGOs, foundations, and the most daring of social investors, a class of "investors" with a strong commitment to the social benefits the extension of a communications infrastructure provides.

The alternative in these developing markets is to force the incumbent, typically monopoly providers, to initiate wireless-based service in unserved areas, thereby imposing on the incumbent a "social tax" earmarked for telecommunications infrastructure development and service provisioning. It is posited, however, that this later approach will always lead to a suboptimal solution for all.

In industrial countries, the issues of bridging the digital divide, of spurring economic development in particular urban and rural areas, or more generally of assuring access to communications services in underserved areas, must find a cost effective solution, and wireless technologies are undoubtedly part of the answer. In developing countries, the very social and economic development of the society as a whole depends critically upon such infrastructure advancement. It falls to us all to work assiduously to assure that the political and regulatory climate reflects these needs, and that institutions step forward that are up to the task. ◑

CASE STUDY COMPENDIUM

Left to their own devices: Twelve developing-world case studies

By Noopur Jhunjhunwala and Peter Orne

THIS CASE STUDY COMPENDIUM SERVES AS A best-practices reference tool for the World Summit on the Information Society. Over the next two years, the Wireless Internet Institute will continue to research and add to an accruing knowledge base focused on growing numbers of wireless Internet deployments throughout the developing world.

The Case Study Compendium presents twelve examples, out of dozens received by the Wireless Internet Institute in the run-up to "The Wireless Internet Opportunity for Developing Countries" conference. To prepare the Compendium, the principle author interviewed project stakeholders, including field practitioners and funders, to present a coherent picture. Each case study was investigated and analyzed using these parameters:

- ▶ mission and goals
- ▶ accomplishments
- ▶ technology used
- ▶ funding sources
- ▶ collaborations
- ▶ regulatory environment
- ▶ expectations vs. outcomes
- ▶ sustainability
- ▶ scalability and replicability

Whether motivated primarily by development objectives, for profit, or for the challenges these projects present, the practitioners shared the goal of bridging the digital divide using broadband wireless technology. Each found a unique solution for overcoming roadblocks, bringing more hope and opportunities to less developed regions.

The case studies group into five categories revealing core aspects of wireless broadband deployments in developing countries:

▶**Remote Regions** provide the harshest environmental test of the technology and of the implementation models.

▶**Wireless Internet Service Providers** are primarily driven by profit but can also contribute to regional development.

▶**Shared Access** provides connectivity to regions that cannot afford individual access.

▶**Adaptive Technologies** rethink off-the-shelf solutions to overcome local limitations.

▶**Rebuilding Nations** can draw from the models above to rebuild a communications infrastructure and jumpstart social and economic development.

In each case study, an analysis box (**Things to Remember**) highlights key aspects, and a schematic (**Network Set-Up**) shows how the network has been or will be deployed. The compendium as a whole raises five sets of issues surrounding deployment of wireless Internet in developing countries.

Why wireless broadband?

Because relatively low investments in equipment can be used to connect a very large area, wireless broadband can be the most affordable last-mile solution available. For two reasons, it is often the only practical solution. Environmental limita-

Noopur Jhunjhunwala is Case Study Manager for the Wireless Internet Institute. Peter Orne is Editor of *The WorldPaper,* World Times, Inc.

tions, such as moving glaciers or deep rainforest interiors, curb the ability to physically lay fiber on the ground. And in some poor countries, where copper or wire are valuable commodities and vulnerable to theft, wireless provides a tamper-proof solution. Moreover, the networks can be deployed quickly, and an administrator can track a problem at any point, enabling fast repair. It's easier to replace an antenna or correct a line-of-sight than to lay new copper or fiber.

Network considerations

The technology in a network is only part of the picture. Critical is how it is set up, what devices are connected to it, and how it is powered. The developed world uses wireless mostly for indoor local area networks, but developing countries are using it largely for outdoor wide area networks. Consequently, in developing countries, practitioners need to improvise with off-the-shelf equipment to widen the coverage area, often with amplifiers. Today, wireless broadband coverage can extend as far as 50 kilometers.

Because equipment used to connect to the network is still expensive, practitioners often must depend on low-end configurations or donated devices, making do until efforts to bring costs below $100 are successful. Another consideration is that extreme temperatures and harsh weather conditions require improvisation.

Availability of power is often taken for granted,

and the cost of having a power-supply back-up can be underestimated. Consequently, systems may go down for long periods, and a project can run over budget. It's important to look at all possible alternatives, such as solar power.

Search for sustainability

Whether the project is for profit or not-for-profit, achieving long-term sustainability can critically depend on local partnerships, hands-on training of local technicians, and buy-in from end users. In a development context, building an understanding of the Internet and awareness of wireless broadband advantages (over existing infrastructures) can generate buy-in from the community. Determine up front the range of needs of end users, involving them from the beginning to create a sense of local ownership.

Shared access through community centers invites a wide range of additional users while leveraging existing infrastructure—and potentially staff—at local post offices and universities. It can also attract nongovernmental organizations and their supportive resource bases.

To move from dependence to self-reliance, the search for sustainability should begin early, with careful thought to potentially generating revenues from the project through small fees for online services and training, or by developing offline projects, such as ecotourism, to subsidize connectivity costs.

In for-profit deployments, it is important, with

some exceptions, not to over-invest and scale up too fast. Let the business grow gradually as new demand is identified, often by word of mouth.

Applications are everything

When people log on to the Internet, they want to communicate, and therefore e-mail and voice and video mail are easily the most popular uses of wireless broadband networks in the developing world. Local people want to get in touch with relatives and friends who may have migrated far distances for employment or education opportunities. The Web can make this easier in a way that national telecoms never could. Internet telephony, or voice-over IP, is also popular in countries where it is permitted.

The Internet's biggest advantage over other communication technologies is that it can provide an array of solutions and products, including the three "e's": e-governance, e-health, e-education (a fourth is e-commerce). Telemonitoring devices enable doctors to diagnose patients living thousands of miles away. Distance education programs teach reading and writing. E-governance initiatives enable villagers to update records and file complaints from their village, saving a day's pay. The list goes on and on.

Like technology, however, applications also face challenges. Local scripts require special software. Illiteracy requires voice solutions. Online services require offline resources—teachers for e-education, doctors and nurses for e-health, payment and

postal systems for e-commerce. The virtual demand chain may be established, but it is meaningless if the offline supply chain is missing.

The regulatory master

Incumbent telecoms in the developing world guard their terrain carefully. In rural areas, which are marginal markets for incumbents, entrepreneurs may face few initial barriers to implementation. In all cases, it is important to know the rules, seek required permits at both local and national levels, and try to bring the incumbent in on the plan, which could enable future scalability.

In cities, the entrepreneur is likely to face the incumbent and regulatory authority head on. Different responses to these entities, however, present varying risks. One is to directly confront telecoms and authorities wholesale, lobbying against them domestically and internationally, which can lead to confiscations, project termination, and even criminal charges. This route requires courage, patience, money, and time.

Another option may simply be to bypass the regulatory environment altogether if the authority is not too aggressive. Still another is to engage in the bureaucratic process, get required permissions, and even try to form an alliance with the incumbent. Authorities may be more convinced by projects with a social-development outcome. A final option is to desist until the regulatory environment changes. But in waiting there is little to be gained. ◐

REMOTE REGIONS

Rising to the challenge

▶Linking Everest, Khumbu Region, Nepal

BRINGING INTERNET ACCESS TO THE BASE CAMP of Mount Everest may well rank among the severest tests of wireless-broadband technology in the world.

Among the well-noted challenges of the Nepalese Himalayas—high altitudes, extremely harsh weather, no roads—is the lack of functional telecommunications infrastructure. The rough mountainous terrain of the Khumbu Region makes deployment of cables extremely difficult and costly. Consequently, wireless broadband is a preferred solution for providing Web and voice-over IP service to both inhabitants and visitors.

But it's not easy achieving and sustaining such service at the base camp to Mt. Everest, which is accessed with a four- to six-day walk from the village of Lukla. Because the altitude is around 5,600 meters, one cannot simply land by helicopter.

There is no power, no buildings, and no infrastructure of any kind in this region. The base camp is located on a glacier that moves about 10 feet each day, prohibiting satellite installation. On top of this, temperatures fall to -20°C at night and can reach 15°C during the day, taxing batteries and electronic components.

The Himalayas, however, are about rising to the challenge. Thanks to a partnership between the Sagarmatha Pollution Control Committee and WorldLink Communications of Nepal, on April 14, 2003 the Linking Everest project did just that. With a goal of operating wireless Internet access for one tourist season, a six-man "Virtual Yeti team" led by Tsering Gyaltsen Sherpa wirelessly linked base camp to a server in Kalapathar using a Cisco Aironet 350, and from there to the Internet via satellite.

THINGS TO REMEMBER

▶Can you imagine digging through a moving glacier to lay fiber? Because of cost, rugged terrain, and deployment logistics, in remote regions wireless connectivity is often the only telecommunications option.

▶In most remote areas, access to basic supplies can delay the connectivity process. For example, in the Khumbu Region, obtaining a single tool can take a four- to six-day walk, cutting into project deployment time and future revenue generation.

▶Regular maintenance is required for smooth and continuous operation of a wireless facility. In Nepal, the technician got altitude sickness, causing the base camp to lose connectivity. Qualified personnel amust be available in a sustainable way.

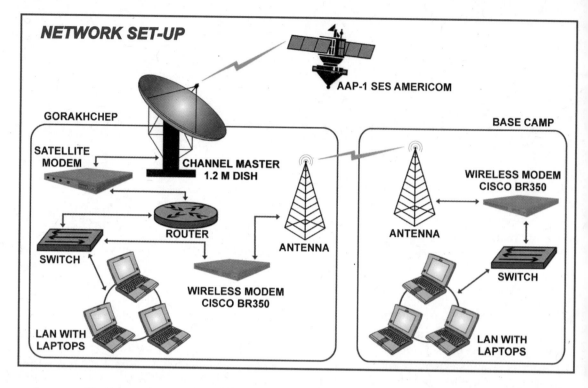

NETWORK SET-UP

AAP-1 SES AMERICOM

GORAKHCHEP

BASE CAMP

SATELLITE MODEM

CHANNEL MASTER 1.2 M DISH

WIRELESS MODEM CISCO BR350

ROUTER

ANTENNA

SWITCH

ANTENNA

WIRELESS MODEM CISCO BR350

SWITCH

LAN WITH LAPTOPS

LAN WITH LAPTOPS

Among other innovations, the team needed to design special Styrofoam cases for outdoor equipment to conserve heat. Bucking conventional wisdom and popular belief, it was able to operate a VSAT terminal on the glacier.

"This isn't commercially motivated," says Dileep Agrawal, founder of WorldLink ISP, which provides capital, equipment, and maintenance for the project. "We got involved because we found it very fascinating. We want to help this community, and we want to prove to the world that we can connect Mt. Everest."

There are two seasons on Everest, and during the second, September 15 to the end of November, the technician manning the base-camp station got altitude sickness and needed to come down, leading to a temporary closure and a revenue shortfall.

"It's all up in the air now," Agrawal reports. "We need a full-time person as a technician." Finding that person is a major barrier to continued success and could kill the hope of sustaining Linking

Everest over the long term. Currently, WorldLink is training a local Sherpa more suited to the base-camp conditions, but low literacy and awareness among the local population are obstacles.

The project has several long-term goals, one of which is to link Namche, the first major settlement on the four-day trek from Lukla to the base camp. In the process, small villages, monasteries, and tourist spots will also be connected and then linked to the Internet using satellite. Expected uses are e-mail and Web access, voice-over IP, distance education, and telemedicine.

At a very basic level, there is a fundamental need among the population to communicate. Many villagers in the region have family in Kathmandu, but government phones aren't easily accessible, and there's never any guarantee they will work. Internet access could enable less reliance not only on the phone system but on the feeble postal service.

Cyber cafés already operate in Namche.

The Virtual Yeti team wirelessly linked Everest base camp at an altitude of 5,600 m to a server in Kalapathar at 5,450 m.

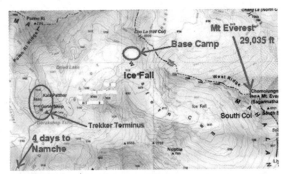

A map of the Khumbu Glacier basin shows the Kalapathar/Gorek Shep area, base camp, and Everest summit.

Tsering Gyaltsen Sherpa logs on wirelessly at Icefall, Everest base camp.

Linking Everest charges $1 per minute at the base camp cyber café.

Currently, an attendant types and sends e-mail for the locals, who seem to have little problem communicating with their relatives. There is an assumption that relatives have access to e-mail. In general, Sherpas who have moved from the region are better off, technically aware and educated.

Proliferating Internet use in the region itself, already traveled with well-heeled tourists, is expected to gradually spur further economic and social development locally. The idea is to charge tourists $1 per minute for Internet use and VoIP and use profits to support local use of the infrastructure during months when tourism slows. During the first tourist season, March 15 to June 1, the project raised $17,532, generating a $10,032 profit after deducting $6,250 for bandwidth and $1,250 for wages and miscellaneous expenses. This revenue was sufficient to pay the operating costs until September 15, when the next tourist season begins.

Dave Hughes, another project supporter, is working to connect the Sir Edmond Hillary School in Namche using wireless broadband. There's also an effort to provide English classes over the Web. One Sherpa who moved to Colorado is trying to give instructions in English.

For now, the Linking Everest team needs once again to reestablish connectivity at base camp, connect the school, and expand its network. But the harsh challenges of the Khumbu Region will continue to test both technology and resolve. ◑

Rainforest IP

▶Xixuaú-Xipariná Ecological Reserve, Jauaperi River, Brazil

INDIVIDUALS AND INSTITUTIONS CONCERNED about the fate of the Amazon and its Indian populations have in recent years begun to lend a helping hand. In the 172,000-hectare Xixuaú-Xipariná Ecological Reserve 40 hours upriver from Manaus, the welfare of the Caboclo Indians is taken very seriously by the Amazon Association, an NGO based in Brazil and Italy that views the Caboclo as key to the preservation of the rainforest.

The Amazon Association has teamed up with the nonprofit Solar Electric Light Fund in Washington, DC, to put broadband Internet at the service of the Indians, who lack access to basic healthcare, education, and economic opportunities. E-mail, telemedicine, online education and even e-commerce promise to radically improve their lives.

Solar panels now power a satellite Internet link in the reserve, which enables the Amazon Association to maintain permanent contact with Indians who have learned to use e-mail, and who can report on problems at the reserve, participate in decision-making, and request supplies and medicines.

"It is important to upgrade the ICT capabilities of the people, and build their knowledge base," says Chris Clark, founding member and current president of the Association.

"The mere ability to communicate on a regular basis with the outside world has provided a tremendous psychological lift to the community there," says Robert Freling of the Solar Electric Light Fund.

Solar energy provides the electricity, a two-way VSAT from OnSat Network Communications

---

THINGS TO REMEMBER

▶Alternate, cheap, and reliable sources of energy often go hand in hand with wireless-network deployment. Because of the total lack of electricity in the rainforest, solar power has been critical to this project.

▶When a project is funded entirely by grants, it is key to work toward sustainability from the very beginning. After the system is up and running, ecotourism and e-commerce may help pay for equipment, maintenance, and expansion.

▶The telemedicine component is a vital-signs monitor loaned to the reserve and administered remotely by US doctors. Consequently, equipment and labor costs could impede scaling this component to other rainforest communities.

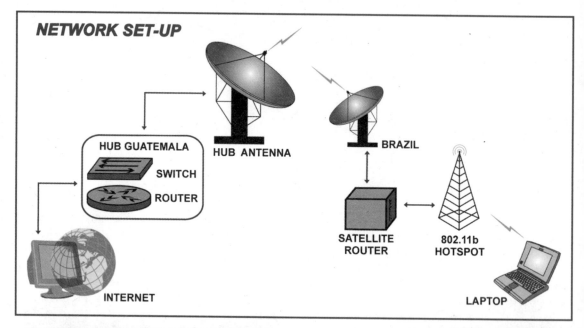

NETWORK SET-UP

HUB GUATEMALA
SWITCH
ROUTER
HUB ANTENNA
BRAZIL
SATELLITE ROUTER
802.11b HOTSPOT
INTERNET
LAPTOP

Grants and good will power the project.

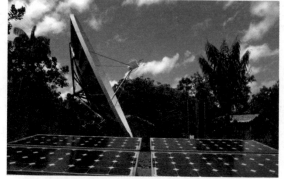

Solar panels power the wireless Internet.

enables high-speed connectivity, and a wireless LAN makes access flexible. The project has applied for a spectrum license from Anatel, Brazil's national telecom.

Of the $75,000 project budget provided by the Ernest Kleinwort Charitable Trust, $50,000 went to hardware and $25,000 to planning, training, and management. The economics of the project, however, remain a serious barrier to growth.

With an eye toward achieving sustainability, a governance board has been set up to collect all rev-enues from the project in a common account and will decide how best to allocate the resources. The project is expected to sustain itself within the next four to five years. It is also setting up a model farm in the reserve so that the community members become more self-sufficient in food production. And there is currently discussion about using solar energy to power a Brazil-nut processing facility in the reserve, which will help generate income for the community.

The project does have a modest e-commerce

In Manaus, minus two computers

"This project was first conceived in November 2000 when Lady Madeleine Kleinwort introduced me to Christopher Clark of the Amazon Association. Working together, we developed a project proposal and submitted it to the Ernest Kleinwort Charitable Trust which awarded funds in June 2001.

"After several months of planning and preparation, equipment was ordered and air shipped to Manaus in late January 2002. I traveled to Manaus with a representative of OnSat Network Communications, a solar technician responsible for installation and training, and a documentary filmmaker. As it turned out, the two Gateway computers we had ordered as part of the shipment had been stolen, but instead of releasing the rest of the cargo, customs officials at the airport in Manaus kept everything locked up. It took an entire week to liberate our shipment, and the whole project almost came to a screeching halt!

"Once the equipment was in our possession, everything was loaded onto a large riverboat

Equipment delivered by river.

Delivery of data by satellite.

owned and operated by the Amazon Association for the 40-hour trip up the Amazon. Because the water level on the Jauaperí River was low at the time, the riverboat was unable to make it all the way to the reserve, so we had to transfer all the equipment onto outboard canoes for the final several miles.

"Altogether, it took four days to install the solar-power equipment, lights, refrigerators, fans, computers, and satellite system in the Xixuaú. Using a Globalstar satphone, Kuen Damiano from OnSat was able to communicate with the satellite operator in Mexico to lock in the signal provided by SatMex V. Shortly thereafter, the wireless LAN was in place, and we were able to send and receive e-mails from the middle of the Amazon rainforest.

"Given availability of additional funding for equipment and training, there is no reason that this project could not be replicated in many other parts of the Brazilian Amazon; indeed throughout the entire developing world, at least on a noncommercial basis."◐

—*Robert Freling*

Remote diagnosis in the Amazon

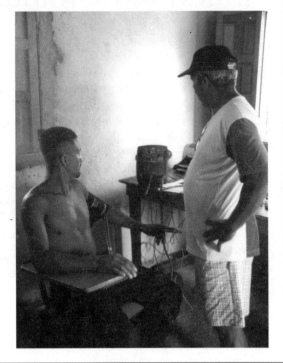

THANKS TO A COLLABORATION WITH THE University of East Carolina Telemedicine Center and the University of South Alabama, the Amazon Association can now use a computer and a vital-signs monitor to remotely take the blood pressure and perform an EKG on the Caboclo Indians, allowing doctors in the US to provide medical consulting and diagnosis.

In one telemedicine experiment just getting under way, a nurse hooks up patients to a "Vital-Link" device which is used to measure the blood pulse, blood pressure, blood oxygen level, body temperature, and EKG of everyone in the community. A doctor at the University of East Carolina Telemedicine Center has control over the machine and can even inflate an armband to take blood pressure. The information is transmitted over the Internet to a doctor, who then videoconferences with the nurse to deliver a diagnosis. ◖◗

component: The women of the local villages have begun taking craftwork orders from foreign visitors guided to the region by the Amazon Association. They recently received a $300 Internet order from an Italian visitor.

The Amazon Association has built three new schools; one is even connected to the Internet. Other projects goals include distance learning, eco-tourism, biodiversity research and mapping. "The plan now," Freeling says, "is to extend connectivity to other communities along the Rio Jauaperí by means of Wi-Fi technology."

"The Association will never abandon this group," says Clark, who has committed to making the reserve and this link to the Caboclo a lifelong project. ◖◗

WIRELESS INTERNET
SERVICE PROVIDERS

Slow incubation success

▶**Africa-Online, Blantyre, Malawi**

MALAWI'S COPPER-BASED TELEPHONE NET-work is often busy and frequently breaks down, and fiber-line use is limited only to areas where economic activity already exists. The country's two cellular operators are far too expensive for general data services or even rural voice services, yet establishing an Internet link in Malawi—the equivalent of a T1 line—can run to $10,000 a month.

These are tough obstacles facing any entrepreneur wishing to deploy a profitable data communications network. But Malawi is also a Least Developed Country, seeming to offer little hope for profitability.

Thanks to wireless infrastructure, however, Africa-Online in Blantyre has managed to provide broadband Internet service in Malawi for more than three years, and it's still going strong. From the outset, the company committed to achieving a return on investment, targeting areas where service could be economically sustainable, such as the economic centers of Blantyre and Lilongwe.

"Conditions are extremely harsh for this type of equipment, and only commercial motivation keeps our network operational and well maintained," says CEO Paul Shaw.

Bandwidth goes from a satellite to customers through Africa-Online's wireless network, requiring careful economic planning in the back office. "We have to pay about 100 times more for bandwidth than an ISP in the United States or Europe," Shaw says. "This alone is the single-most important factor in modeling the business and has a massive downstream effect on our market."

Shaw estimates Africa-Online's current value at $500,000, as a going concern, after an initial shareholder investment of $100,000. No dividend has been paid, and all earnings have been ploughed back into the company. Africa-Online is the only one of four to five ISPs in Malawi providing full-

---

THINGS TO REMEMBER

▶It is important not to over-invest and outpace demand by expanding too rapidly. Africa-Online emphasizes the virtues of starting small and growing organically for the long term.

▶Installing technology is not enough. It is important to reserve resources for training customers how to use it.

▶A wireless connection cannot be stolen. Where copper-wire infrastructure is routinely resold as raw material, wireless proves its advantage in Malawi as it does in rugged or mountainous terrain.

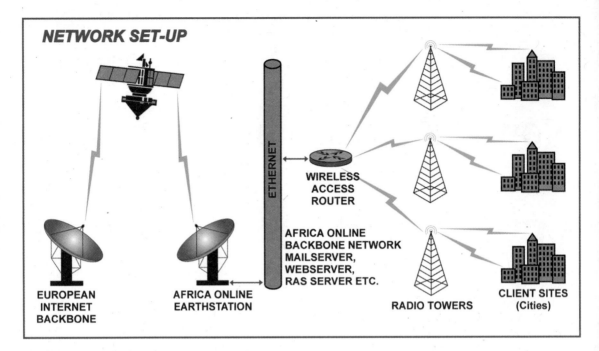

NETWORK SET-UP

EUROPEAN INTERNET BACKBONE

AFRICA ONLINE EARTHSTATION

ETHERNET

WIRELESS ACCESS ROUTER

AFRICA ONLINE BACKBONE NETWORK MAILSERVER, WEBSERVER, RAS SERVER ETC.

RADIO TOWERS

CLIENT SITES (Cities)

time wireless access to 200 of its 2,000 subscribers (most of whom are dial-up).

Africa-Online says the secret to success is starting small and growing organically, mostly by word of mouth, making minimum investments for minimum returns. "Major investment in high-tech equipment in developing countries is a sure-fire road to disaster," Shaw says. "It is not practical to create an infrastructure and then wait for clients to line up to use it. Allow years for the learning curve to kick in."

Africa-Online found it had to provide networking installation and services, routing and switching services, and training on mail exchange and firewalls. "It is not enough to facilitate the installation of a specific technology; you have to support all aspects and uses of that technology and be able to do it on a commercially sustainable basis," Shaw says.

He says it is important to take great care in selecting equipment, and not to assume the industry standard is the best in every circumstance. Africa-Online uses Alvarion BreezeNet equipment. "Alvarion provided initial training but we had to improvise," Shaw says. If equipment fails,

Africa-Online will replace it for no cost through the Israeli manufacturer.

Incubating economic development

Seventy percent of Africa-Online clients are commercial, and Shaw says he has seen a positive impact from broadband services on Malawi's corporate and banking sectors. High-speed Internet access has brought confidence to external investors and helped rural agricultural clients, for example, get access to commodity pricing to maximize their returns. Because of the poor state of the telephone network, e-mail is now the primary medium for doing business with both national and international clients.

"Clients first want e-mail connectivity, then want to be able to research their businesses, and lastly the businesses want to have a presence on the Internet so they can get some sort of economic return from this," Shaw says.

Some businesses with Web sites hosted by Africa-Online have begun to increase their exports because of their ability to take online orders. At least two agri-

Africa-Online enjoys new offices in Blantyre.

The company originated in 2000 in this A-frame.

It has connected a local backpacker lodge.

Africa-Online's installation for an Internet café.

cultural organizations are exporting tea and coffee by selling and shipping directly to customers in Kenya, the UK, and South Africa. While the Internet mostly benefits large farmers who can afford to finance shipping and absorb payment delays, the hope is that small-scale farmers will form cooperatives and benefit from their own Web presence.

Africa-Online offers residential users discount rates at night (6:00 pm to 6:00 am) at a fraction of the normal cost. If regulators approve, the company will gradually move into voice-over IP. The regulatory position on VoIP is less clear but has not been ruled out. The ISM bands are available for use after payment of a registration fee.

While it has not brought Internet access to the urban or rural poor, Africa-Online has given donors

and NGOs access to better and more efficient technologies, assisting them in the delivery of development solutions. "We can see that the introduction of full-time access to the Internet has led to greater knowledge being available in the community at large and increasing interest in our services," Shaw says.

An agricultural concern has queried the company about providing connectivity to a farming area in the south of Malawi, given that the state telecom only offers a 19.2 Kbps analog connection. Africa-Online will consider expanding to rural areas where willing entrepreneurs could run cyber cafes. In addition, they have proposed connecting Malawi's postal service, replacing telex with e-mail, and replacing a "letter writer" with an "email typist" in every village. ◑

Paul Shaw on beating the backhaul cost

PROVIDING BROADBAND IN A LEAST DEVELOPED Country with fewer numbers of subscribers requires a careful study, says Africa-Online CEO Paul Shaw. It's not just about providing an affordable last-mile solution.

"For a symmetrical T1 leased-line connection to the Internet in the United States, prices vary from $750 in, say, California to $1,000 in rural areas. But that same bandwidth in Africa can cost from $24,000 to $55,000. If I am lucky enough to be living in a country that allows me to use my own satellite equipment, then my costs are at the lower end of that scale.

"But there are many countries in Africa where dedicated bandwidth is not even available and shared bandwidth must be used with a resulting decrease in quality—though not much of a decrease in price. The cost of leased lines to customers, or to peering points, is also many times more expensive.

"On the income side, the picture is just as bleak. My company charges $35 per month for an unlimited-access dial-up connection, for example. Considering that my input costs are 30 times greater than an ISP in the United States, that does not compare badly.

"Market sizes are not large. There are only 1,600,000 dial-up subscribers in all of Africa, and hardly any cable or DSL subscribers, largely because of the extortionately high telecom costs. There's very low average income—$1,600 per capita per year—in sub-Saharan Africa, and very low teledensity and low literacy rates.

"On the teledensity issue, Kenya, one of the most Internet-active countries in Africa, only had a total of some 450,000 lines installed. Ghana has 250,000, a lot less than a large town or small city in the United States.

Fighting for users

"In Africa, a big ISP has a few hundred thousand dial-up subscribers, or a few hundred leased lines. There are only a handful of these, maybe three. For the majority of African ISPs, 1,000 subscribers is a lot. In Mbps, here are the numbers for international bandwidth (2002) by country:

Egypt	535
South Africa *	399
Morocco	136
Algeria	83
Tunisia	75
Senegal*	60
Kenya*	28
Gabon*	16
Nigeria*	15
Botswana*	14

*Sub-Saharan Africa

"The remaining countries have less than 13 Mbps each, with Equatorial Guinea at the bottom of the list with 64 kbps for half a million people. An average ISP in the United States probably has more bandwidth than many of the countries on this list.

"The high cost, relative to income, of being an Internet subscriber in Africa means that many ISPs must share a very small number of subscribers. The high cost of operating as an ISP in Africa means that margins are small to nonexistent, and that it's impossible to expand the way you'd like.

"Finally, there is the "Half Way Proposal" (see http://www.afrispa.org/initiatives.htm), which compares Internet provision with voice provision. When an international call is placed from the United States to Malawi and another from Malawi to the United States, the two telecoms involved have a monthly settlement arrangement where the cost of terminating the calls is taken into account. Because far more calls terminate in Malawi than originate there, this monthly settlement is a major source of revenue for the telecom and of foreign exchange for Malawi. When an e-mail is sent from the United States to Malawi or from Malawi to the United States, the entire cost of transit, in either direction, is born by the African ISP." ⑩

Making it at the margins

▶Baja Wireless, Ensenada, Mexico

THE SMALLER CITIES OF MEXICO STILL LACK reliable access to basic telecommunications, let alone fast Internet access. Only 44 percent of Mexico's population has a landline, and it can take Telmex, the national telecom, up to nine months to install basic fixed-line service in certain areas.

But with Internet activity booming in Mexico's large cities and in the nearby United States, and with computer use growing everywhere, smaller working cities—marginal markets with a good mix of residential, industrial, and commercial activity—are understandably thirsty for broadband access.

In a prototype operation in Ensenada, about 65 miles south of San Diego, Baja Wireless is delivering connectivity via a 7,500-acre hot zone. With an ultimate goal of connecting about 30 cities in the next 30 months, this wireless ISP is targeting small cities with 50,000 to 500,000 residents who may have no wired telephone service because of backlog, who want or need improved Internet access speed, or who simply want the convenience of wireless Internet access. Baja Wireless offers different packages for clients based on their bandwidth usage.

The business model met with skepticism at first. "Baja Wireless repeatedly heard howls or blank stares of disbelief at the thought that anybody might be interested in investing in a telecommunications project in Mexico," says cofounder Sharron Tate, an American. "Relatively few people could see beyond the risk of investing in a foreign, if neighboring, country." Today, the company claims $300,000 in private investment.

After reaching its first 100 customers, Baja Wireless determined that its Alvarion hardware was cost prohibitive for the mass market in Mexico, so it switched to less expensive D-Link units and met with great success over large distances and uneven terrain. The switch, however, cost the company a four-month delay, draining capital and imparting a valuable lesson. "Identify sources for more capital than you think you will ever need," Tate says. "The unexpected always appears, so be prepared for it."

THINGS TO REMEMBER

▶One way to deal with a strong incumbent monopoly is to deploy in marginal markets where the incumbent's revenue stream is not affected. This might even make collaborating with the monopoly for potential support and future scaling possible.

▶Choose equipment carefully. Baja Wireless's switch from Alvarion to D-Link resulted in better performance at a lower cost, but the transition drained capital and slowed expansion.

NETWORK SET-UP

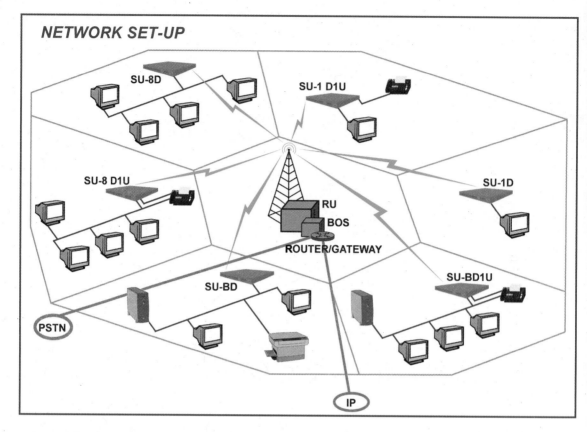

In addition to e-mail communication, Baja Wireless anticipates a range of uses across its network. A doctor in Ensenada can now share X-rays with a colleague at Stanford Medical Center, which was previously very difficult at dial-up speed. Cash-based businesses can install wireless Webcams to remotely watch cash drawers, and manufacturers can monitor manufacturing activities.

In the incumbent's back yard

Baja Wireless describes the regulatory environment in Mexico as "somewhat stringent." Yet, Telmex, one of the world's most powerful telecom monopolies, has encouraged its activities. "They've been extremely supportive and appreciative and are doing everything to help this initiative," says cofounder Tracy Blackett.

While Baja Wireless is a licensed ISP, it is pro-

hibited in Mexico from promoting or providing voice-over IP. Telmex charges $.87 per minute to place a call to the United States and requires other long-distance operators to charge similarly high rates.

"This is a limitation we have," Tate says. "But Baja Wireless got in under the wire just two weeks before licensing requirements tightened in Mexico." Anticipating the company's growth to other towns and regions, it has contracted with Telmex to use a wireless local loop. In this way, the goliath monopoly becomes part of their overall solution.

Costly bandwidth arrives at Baja Wireless's office through Telmex, which receives it from Sprint at the US-Mexico border. "In the United States, we would pay $300 to $500 a month," Blackett says. "Here we pay $2,500 a month for a connection which is 25 percent greater bandwidth than a T1." ◑

It takes a hemisphere

▶E-link Americas

WIRELESS INTERNET SERVICE PROVIDERS at work in regions with insufficient backbone connectivity often struggle with slow growth. Because broadband connectivity costs are high and revenues are slow to come, it is important not to scale up too quickly and run the risk of over-investment.

But a public-private partnership called E-Link Americas is convinced that a broad-scale deployment of wireless broadband is a better model, thanks to new satellite technology—so-called broadband in the sky—that may make it possible to leverage economies of scale and dramatically lower Internet access fees across vast regions of the developing world.

"There's a specific problem that needs to be solved in the Americas, which is low-cost access in rural areas," says Randy Zadra, Managing Director of the Institute for Connectivity of the Americas, or ICA, in Ottawa—one of the funders of the project along with the World Bank, the Organization of American States, and several satellite companies. "Picture doctors going to small clinics where they barely have a phone line. This is a medical intern in his 20s, who's extremely computer literate, who has keyboard skills, and would love nothing better than to have the Internet in front of him so he can see pictures of problems he faces in order to cure people, and use the Internet to continue his training." A market assessment by Era Digital found that only 3 percent of more than 10,000 rural medical clinics in the Americas had Internet access.

E-Link is banking on DVB-RCS—Digital Video Broadcasting Return Channel via Satellite—which was recently published as an ETSI stan-

---

THINGS TO REMEMBER

▶E-Link Americas turns the "small-scale struggle" for deployment on its head. However, while its principle aim is broad-scale deployment to leverage economies of scale, at press time it had not lined up a single customer on the ground.

▶E-Link's success rests with a long chain of partners, from funders to hardware vendors to local ISPs. While partnerships are extremely important for smooth functioning of any network, for a project of this scale the amount of planning has delayed time to deployment.

▶E-Link is opting for open-standards technology to push down costs and encourage rapid technology advancement.

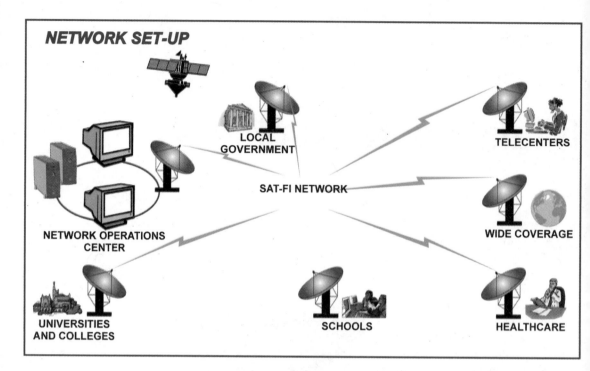

NETWORK SET-UP

LOCAL GOVERNMENT

SAT-FI NETWORK

TELECENTERS

WIDE COVERAGE

NETWORK OPERATIONS CENTER

UNIVERSITIES AND COLLEGES

SCHOOLS

HEALTHCARE

dard, to serve a range of potential customers on a regional (not country) basis throughout the Americas, in order to leverage economies of scale.

DVB-RCS is both cost efficient and scalable. A simple, single-gateway DVB-RCS system can serve up to thousands of users, while a distributed gateway architecture DVB-RCS system could provide integrated services to several hundred thousand users. Customers with small antenna terminals (80 to 90 cm in diameter) get high-speed Internet access through high-frequency bands, multi-spot coverage areas, and high-speed digital signal processing on board the satellite.

Where connectivity was once achieved on a piecemeal basis (with a single satellite beam), E-Link will connect large numbers of institutions and telecenters at a rate of 256 Kbps to 2 Mbps for only $75 to $150 per month. It is aiming at generic markets such as health centers (largely scattered in rural areas), smaller municipalities and institutions outside major urban areas with no connectivity, telecenters, and schools. While coverage will be avail-

able throughout a region, connectivity will be provided regionally through local ISP and IT partners.

"What happened in the world is that solutions to deploy satellites have been proprietary," Zadra says. "This is not cost effective and it doesn't scale. You are held captive to prices and controls that only one company can provide. But with open-standards technology, any company that can provide the specifications of the open standards can supply for us."

Because it allows hardware manufacturers to focus on a single technical solution, DVB-RCS may well become a global satellite standard, providing a healthy and open competitive environment that benefits both industry and users.

"As we've seen with Wi-Fi, you get a lot of hardware producers that push the cost down," Zadra says.

E-Link ultimately remains not a satellite solution but a wireless solution, bundling both satellite and Wi-Fi together. It wants to put a Wi-Fi chip in the satellite so the last mile becomes an 802.11

solution, further lowering costs.

The partner chain

E-Link works through a partnership among satellite, hardware, and funding interests as well as incumbent carriers (who can help ensure scalability further on). Each partner rolls out a different piece of the initial deployment.

"If you bundle the capacities of the different pieces that need to be integrated to provide a solution, then you have a little more cost-effective way to provide it," Zadra says. "We have more equipment vendors than are required. We have more satellite proposals than required. It is a good position to be in because we are trying to determine what options provide the best value proposition."

E-Link is a for-profit company that is essentially owned by a nonprofit trust, which disburses funds to E-Link which then provides the services and takes in revenues. Equipment maintenance is done by E-Link value-added service providers, which differ from country to country. In each case, local partners handle deployments, mainte-

nance, and support.

E-link has a threefold strategy to tackle the different regulatory environments among the many countries of the Americas. It intends to work with within-country value-added partners who are already licensed to provide Internet service. Where regulatory impediments arise, it will ask governments and ministers for special exemptions to ensure that, for example, schools can be served. In some instances, it may work to change legislation (though E-Link acknowledges that that this approach is time intensive and could take years). E-Link plans to extend service first to those countries with no regulatory restrictions to DVB-IP and Wi-Fi, such as Brazil, parts of the Caribbean, Chile, and Mexico.

While actual deployment still lies the future, Zadra says "the issue is getting it right, and not the demand." Deployment rests on a network of local country-specific partnerships, and E-Link needs everything lined up correctly. It is aiming toward the Caribbean and Central America for its first phase of deployment and will move on from there. ◑

WISP on the edge

▶**UniNet Communications, Cape Town, South Africa**

UNINET COMMUNICATIONS OF CAPE TOWN is an ISP with 11 employees committed to providing cheaper last-mile connectivity for home professionals and small businesses in urban areas and to those living in isolation in rural areas. CEO David Jarvis first launched the business in Mozambique, using wireless broadband to provide a more affordable last-mile solution for customers.

"The service offered by the existing monopolies in Mozambique and South Africa is of variable quality and very expensive," Jarvis says. "They are also often unable or unwilling to cover disadvantaged areas."

In Cape Town, a wealthy urban area, UniNet is working on a phased approach of targeting certain kinds of clients, first to get the company up and running and then to expand to rural and disadvantaged areas later on.

"Unlike most larger companies, we see real long-term commercial potential in the rural under-developed sectors of the society," Jarvis says. "With wireless technologies, we can afford to establish hotspots in rural areas by focusing on community centers such as local schools."

Jarvis believes the support for rural and disadvantaged areas can be done through contracts with government departments or with the support of NGOs. He said aid organizations are keen to support initiatives that deliver communications into rural areas, providing the initial impetus to establish new services there.

UniNet, for example, has closely investigated telecenters run by the University Eduardo Mondlane in Mozambique. This university has a proactive IT section, and the university runs its own 802.11 wireless backbone across Maputo city.

The challenge from regulators

Jarvis set up UniNet Lda, the first wireless ISP in Mozambique. In South Africa, UniNet along with FrogFoot Networks has designed and manu-

---

THINGS TO REMEMBER

▶Taking bold steps to confront regulators could help push needed reforms. Adding international pressure also helps. Remember, that extensive openness about your own services can harm your operation and result in equipment confiscation.
▶At every turn, equipment may need to be modified to meet the needs of the local environment.
▶As a last-mile solution, wireless broadband networks are cheap and reliable, can be deployed quickly, and expanded easily.

NETWORK SET-UP

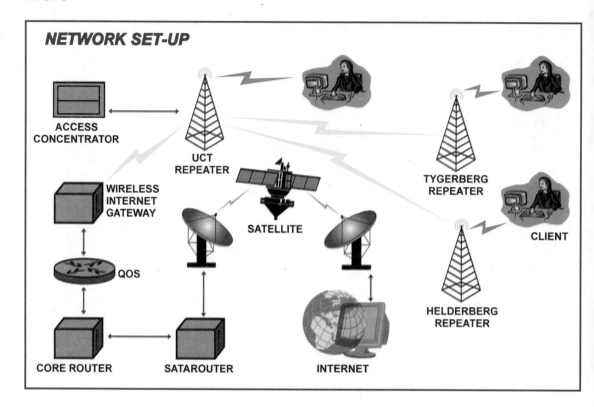

factured its own antenna systems, and built its own Linux-based access concentrators and wireless repeaters. It has tested a range of wireless radios and cabling systems and refined its requirements to ensure reliability and cost effectiveness in a developing environment. And it has used solar-powered installations because of the unreliable electricity grid and the rural location of some of its sites.

In both Mozambique and South Africa, however, UniNet's activities have threatened state monopolies, resulting in a series of challenges from these countries' regulatory agencies.

"The big state-owned telecommunications companies are still trying to keep their monopoly," Jarvis says. "The rules and regulations are not well defined, and this is generally used to help protect the existing monopolies."

In Mozambique, the National Institute of Communications, the regulatory authority, told

UniNet it must suspend all services running on 2.4 Ghz. But after some legal consultation, UniNet found there were no regulations for this area of communications services. UniNet resolved to request formal documentation stating the requirements for licensing its service, and why it was not legal to continue. But with no formal document forthcoming, it decided to continue on.

Jarvis's experiences in Mozambique gave him the confidence to tackle the South African market, where the Independent Communications Authority of South Africa, or ICASA, is far more organized and active. "The main barrier at the moment is the regulatory authority," Jarvis says. "A clear understanding of the legal framework, and the attitudes of the local regulatory authority are crucial."

Cape Town controllers

In July 2002, with an initial investment of $28,000 from its three owners, UniNet began

In Cape Town, an ICASA technician disassembles UniNet equipment. In the center photo, CEO David Jarvis tries to prevent any damage.

building a wireless ISP in Cape Town—just enough to establish one repeater on a high site. "From there we expanded and self-financed the second repeater site," Jarvis says. But before long, ICASA called on the tiny start-up.

"They have repeatedly threatened to close us down and recently confiscated some of our equipment from a high site," Jarvis says.

There are currently five other wireless ISPs operating in the city. UniNet has 73 clients connected to its network, 20 of whom were temporarily disconnected because of the confiscation of equipment at one of its high sites.

In the future, Jarvis says he probably would not expose UniNet so much. "We were very open with regard to location of our repeaters, the type of technology used, and coverage areas. This made it easier for the regulatory authority to locate our equipment and facilitated its attempts to investigate our services."

UniNet has presented proposals to other licensed telecommunications operators, in the hope of generating interest for a buy-in to help "license" its wireless Internet activities. It is currently awaiting responses to these proposals. UniNet has also been seeking international support for its regulatory difficulties with ICASA. It has approached USAID, the World Bank, and local government departments in an attempt to lobby support for the deregulation process.

"This process is slowly gaining momentum," Jarvis says, "but we still often feel very vulnerable in the context of these restrictive regulatory frameworks." ◑

Going head to head with regulators

WITH THE EXCEPTION OF PRIVATE CORporate use within certain boundaries, commercial wireless broadband activity has historically been viewed as illegal within the scope of South Africa's Telecoms Act, according to sources within South Africa's Independent Communications Authority. ICASA has no formal position on the legality of Wi-Fi "outdoor" services. Nevertheless, it has confiscated equipment on three occasions, disrupting the operation of UniNet's network.

CEO David Jarvis says that ICASA seems to have withdrawn its legal processes against companies like his and backed off from what he calls its "aggressive attitudes."

Q. What has ICASA been specifically concerned about?

A. We have been running the networks in the license-free frequencies, 2.4 Ghz and 5.8 Ghz, but the regulator is unhappy with our existing license. ICASA is concerned that we are providing not only a telecommunications service but also our own infrastructure across "public roads"—in other words, we fall into the category of infrastructure provider.

Q. Describe the telecoms legal landscape as 2003 draws to a close.

A. At the moment, the framework is changing tremendously. The government is encouraging a very rapid reform process and introduction of a convergence bill in the course of next year. Among other things, this law will empower a number of other companies to offer services similar to those of the state monopoly.

Q. How does wireless broadband fit in?

A. Wi-Fi falls into this category to some extent, but there is vagueness about exactly how the new bill will interpret its use. There is a move to limit Wi-Fi to indoor use and/or only on a single premises, which unfortunately means that then Wi-Fi will be limited to the domain of developed areas and not developing areas.

Q. What about the competition?

A. About 15 companies in South Africa operate public outdoor Wi-Fi networks, and there is little collaboration among them, because most of the companies are operating quasi-underground. In the Western Cape, however, operators have formed a wireless Internet exchange, WINX, which serves as a platform for collaboration. Frequency planning and strategies for surviving harassment by the regulator are common points of discussion.

Q. Where does UniNet stand in the range of wireless broadband providers?

A. We are by no means a major player, but we've had significant interaction with the regulator because of confiscations. This is partly because we made it easy for the regulator to make an example of us. We were very public in our advertising. Our Web site is very descriptive and informative and open regarding the services we were providing, and our prices were competitive.

Q. How exactly did you get into trouble?

A. The regulator was encouraged by the state monopoly to act against us before we made substantial inroads into their market. In South Africa, the regulator does not work on its own. It acts on complaints from an operator. We have received threatening letters from the operator, saying they will use legal means to recover lost revenues if we do not cease operations.

It's ironic. The municipalities here have wireless networks that connect all their office buildings, yet the government, through ICASA, is not supportive. In effect, the municipalities are fighting the government. ◐

SHARED ACCESS

Scaling Africa's ivory towers

▶**Partners in Education, Saint Louis, Senegal; Njoro, Kenya**

A
S RURAL UNIVERSITIES IN AFRICA GRADUALLY acquire Internet access, they can begin bringing social and economic opportunities to the communities that surround them. The universities can build cyber centers linking (often wirelessly) beyond their walls to help pay connectivity costs, and the centers themselves can begin to meet local development needs.

Over the past couple of years, the John W. McCormack Graduate School of Policy Studies at the UMass Boston has partnered with universities in Senegal and Kenya to build such university-oriented operations.

"Normally, the universities are gated," says Margery O'Donnell, Project Administrator with the McCormack Graduate School. "What this is doing is reorienting the thinking of the universities' people to help surrounding community development."

McCormack's community resource centers, or CRCs, are much more than cyber cafés, which simply help make the centers self-sustaining. They're being furnished with business-center equipment and other components to serve the development needs of the general population and at-risk youth.

The central idea is to build the CRC, funded by USAID's Education for Development and Democracy Initiative, and then adapt the social and economic programs to meet the needs of the community and of NGOs interested in working in the area. The potential for each CRC is virtually unlimited and rests with the imagination of the local community.

Senegal and Kenya

McCormack's first partnership was in rural Northern Senegal with Université Gaston Berger de Saint-Louis, whose Internet link enabled

---

THINGS TO REMEMBER

▶The McCormack Institute partnerships are primarily interested in bringing social and economic development opportunities to rural areas. They've chosen technology and a wireless solution to achieve these goals, but don't view connectivity alone as a final objective. While the Internet has been critical to providing distance education in Masaailand, in Senegal it has been used to generate returns through a cyber café.

▶The partnerships are both replicable, from Senegal to Kenya, and scalable, within Kenya.

▶These deployments take best advantage of an untapped local resource: existing university infrastructure.

McCormack to wirelessly connect a newly constructed CRC one fourth of a mile from the university. The CRC has a business center with a fax machine and a cyber café generating income to sustain overall operations. But there's also a women's center, sewing workshop, classrooms, and associated agricultural and transport initiatives.

Because of its success in Senegal, the Institute pushed on to rural Egerton University in Njoro, Kenya, 112 miles northwest of Nairobi. At Egerton, the deployment began by installing a computer lab in the university. (While USAID has connected universities in Kenya with fiber, the Faculty of Arts and Social Sciences had only one computer.) Here, the CRC is being built only half a mile from the gated campus where the Internet connection to the university has been made with fiber. As the CRC is built, the mentoring programs and online distance learning will be conducted at the university.

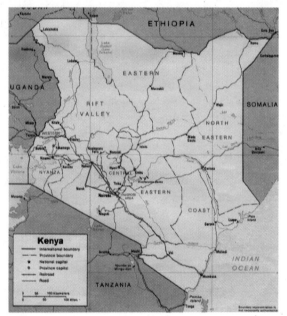

McCormack project locations in Kenya.

Because of the AIDS crisis in Kenya, the Njoro CRC has a special mission: "Basically, any programs that you can think of relating to AIDS will be here," O'Donnell says. This includes testing for the virus [Voluntary Counseling and Testing (VCTs)], education, mitigation, awareness, and mentoring of young people. Social and economic development programs will help to remove the stigma and ostracization of those affected by HIV/AIDS, reintegrating them back into the community. Programs will deal with the AIDS orphan crisis (2.1 million in Kenya) and grandmothers who are the caretakers of those orphans. A dispensary and pharmacy are also planned.

The First Lady of Kenya is chairing a board developed by the Institue that will help to establish this model countrywide. Long after AIDS has been eradicated in Kenya, the CRCs with their IT capacity will still be standing.

Maasailand

McCormack is now scaling its Njoro operation to an unserved Maasailand community 75 miles to the south of Egerton University in Narok. The $83,000 project will bring Internet-based distance education to Narok's Maasai Education Discovery, a fledging CRC working to serve Maasai youth and to help create economic development opportunities.

The effort here especially targets Maasai girls, who are deprived of any education opportunities. "Maybe one Maasai girl goes to university each year," O'Donnell says. "Most are married young and have many babies." About 80 students from Maasailand and Egerton have already been enrolled into distance-education classes to be provided by UMass Boston beginning in January 2004.

Because connecting the Maasai Education Discovery has been expensive, the Institute has been debating whether to link it to the Internet using a satellite or a wireless link back to Egerton.

"The problem with a landline is that it's just not going to work in the hinterland of Sub-Saharan Africa," O'Donnell says. "When the CRC

The Saint-Louis CRC in Senegal.

The Saint-Louis CRC computer lab.

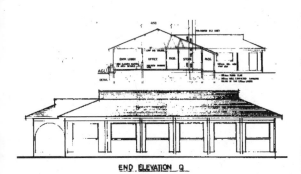
Plans for Egerton CRC in Kenya.

Maasai Education Discovery in Njorok.

is near the university we can lay the lines, but once the CRCs are father away, we need to consider wireless options."

In October 2003, additional funds were raised for the Narok project to purchase a DVB-RCS, or Digital Video Broadcaster and Receiver, for a one-time cost of $10,000. Its wireless antenna has a 7-km radius which can reach computers newly installed in local Maasailand schools. The monthly usage, however, is $2,000, and the schools are expected to chip in. "This is an extraordinary step here in Kenya," O'Donnell says.

So far, McCormack has not hit any substantial regulatory barriers in Senegal or Kenya. While both countries have been privatizing, "it doesn't mean that if we received a billion dollars and want to put wireless all over Kenya that we will not have a problem," O'Donnell says. "We're finding a way on the ground here. It takes small projects like this to become important."

O'Donnell would like to see the spread of CRCs throughout Kenya's university system. Kenya has an AIDS mandate, and the First Lady has expressed an interest in further expansion of the Egerton project. This CRC model in Kenya could be used elsewhere in Africa to deal with the AIDS pandemic.

"We are trying to break the back of the digital divide," O'Donnell says, "so however we can do it, we will." ◑

Village replication

▶**Sustainable Access in Rural India, Tamil Nadu State, India**

IN A 2,000-SQ-KM AREA THAT IS HOME TO 32,000 Indians, Sustainable Access in Rural India, or SARI, has helped 23 percent of the population connect to the Internet—remarkable, given India's overall average of 1.5 percent and a worldwide average of 9 percent.

In this pilot project, applications and content are provided wirelessly to more than 80 sites in 50 villages in Madurai District, in Tamil Nadu State, which equates to the highest density of rural Internet kiosks anywhere in the world.

SARI is a public, private, and academic collaboration among IIT in Madras, Harvard's Berkman Center for Internet & Society, MIT's Program on Internet & Telecoms Convergence, and the I-Gyan

Foundation. n-Logue Communications Pvt. Ltd. is the private-sector implementing partner.

The idea is to tap India's relatively well-laid fiber infrastructure, which penetrates most towns, and bring low-cost connectivity to surrounding villages. SARI uses corDECT, a wireless local loop developed by IIT, which currently costs around $320 but should ultimately drop to $200.

n-Logue, the project driver, works together entrepreneurially with a start-up local Internet service provider and village kiosk operators to provide connectivity and services. The LSP in this case co-invests with n-Logue to sell connectivity to a radius of about 35 km (generally a couple of small towns and about 350 villages). The average size of

---

THINGS TO REMEMBER

▶Multiple partners bring a range of perspectives and widen the range of available services.
▶Users usually need to see a clear benefit to new technology before they will use it. A proactive telekiosk operator can build trust in the technology while pushing applications.
▶Everyone must benefit. Villagers receive services and kiosk operators and LSPs earn profits—a typical win-win situation enabling scaling to and replication in other regions.
▶The LSP provides valuable structured training for maintenance and applications, helping the kiosk operator buy into the project.
▶n-Logue's approach is top down, whereas in Africa the McCormack Institute relies on the community to drive project agenda. At Egerton University, IT is but one tool. In SARI, it is the only tool.
▶Phones in every home are not affordable, so shared access is fundamental to project start-up and growth.

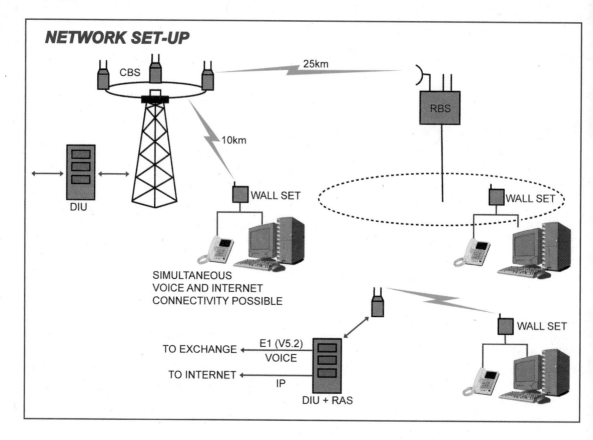

NETWORK SET-UP

CBS

25km

RBS

10km

DIU

WALL SET

WALL SET

SIMULTANEOUS
VOICE AND INTERNET
CONNECTIVITY POSSIBLE

WALL SET

TO EXCHANGE ← E1 (V5.2)
VOICE

TO INTERNET ←
IP

DIU + RAS

a village with a telekiosk is 1,000 households, while the smallest villages have fewer than 300 households. Average per-capita income is under $1 a day.

With a $1,000 loan from a village bank—the maximum amount allowed at that branch level— the kiosk operator invests in a basic kit that includes the wireless connection, a multimedia PC with a color monitor, multimedia equipment and web camera, a power source with a four-hour back-up battery, and a dot-matrix printer.

The LSP trains the kiosk operators, usually young men and women from the villages, providing them with software support and technical skills. The kiosk operators then maintain the equipment and assist customers in sending and retrieving voice and text messages, filling in online forms, and using the Web. Above all, these com-

puter-literate early adopters communicate the potential benefits of the telekiosk to the villagers in an understandable and appealing way.

To break even, the operator must generate $3 per day, charging a minimum fee for each service to pay off the loan and begin making a profit. The operator must be willing to win the trust of new users, going the extra length to create awareness and encourage computer usage in order to increase revenues.

The first telekiosks were installed in November 2001, and to date, about a quarter are breaking even or are profitable. Telekiosks in larger villages seem to generate better returns simply because there are more users there. Early services include communications, education and training, tele-agriculture, tele-medicine, entertainment, and e-government.

Because the infrastructure investments by the LSP are relatively low (averaging about $75,000

An infinity of applications

BECAUSE VILLAGERS NEED TO BE CONVINCED that paying for Internet services will benefit them, SARI's success depends on telekiosk operators building trust among users and pushing a variety of applications (generally tailored for low literacy in English) in five categories: communication, wealth, entertainment, education, and e-governance. Each can generate revenues for the operator and benefit the villager.

Because many friends and relatives in Tamil Nadu have emigrated to the Gulf and other regions in search of jobs, the e-mail, voice, and video mail services provided are very useful. Voice and video conferencing have enabled families separated by great distances to communicate regularly.

In one example, a woman's kidneys failed after her husband left for the Gulf. Hearing this, her in-laws sent her back to her parents, disowning her and saying she was defective. This woman managed to get a kidney transplant, but her in-laws refused to take her back into the family, and when she asked how to contact her husband, they would not give her the information. She managed to obtain his contact through a friend. The husband was sent a letter explaining how to obtain an e-mail account and a time was set to videoconference. Sitting thousands of miles away, the husband was made aware of the real situation.

Thanks to e-governance applications, villagers can now send online applications for pensions, birth, death, below-poverty-line, and encumbrance certificates; register complaints of broken street lights and drinking-water problems; and send petitions to government politicians and bureaucrats, allowing interaction at five different levels of government.

In Tamil Nadu, the cost to a villager when applying for a birth certificate online drops from the usual $6 to $2. A handicapped villager who lost his job managing the local water pump because of "local politics" petitioned the chief minister by e-mail and was subsequently rein-

COMMUNICATION — Save time / Save money

E-GOVERNANCE — Easy access / Reduce middlemen

WEALTH — Reduce costs / Increase yield / Better health

CUSTOMER

EDUCATION — Increase literacy levels / Augment school education

ENTERTAINMENT — Movies / Music / Photography

stated. At least two such petitions are sent each month. A village president who was abusing her position of authority to sell publicly owned trees was removed after e-mail complaints from the local kiosk operator.

SARI has collaborated with the local agricultural college to provide online consultations by e-mail and video conferencing, because small farmers can turn only to pesticide suppliers or their peers for advice. Some 45 specific inquiries were received from farmers in just four months through the kiosk's tele-agriculture service. In one case, a farmer avoided losing a $2,800 diseased okra crop after receiving, ▶

per district) and an entire village kiosk set-up costs approximately $1,000, SARI appears to be highly scalable. An investment of less than $100,000 per district can be leveraged six or seven times with local funding from the LSP and kiosk operators.

Consequently, SARI has been replicated in 7 other Indian states through 16 more projects. The current goal is to roll out SARI to 30,000 villages over the next two years, and to cover over 500,000 villages in the next three to four years, providing access to 85 percent of the rural Indian population.

Going forward, research teams from IIT Madras, MIT, and Harvard University, working with a range of local collaborators, will explore new technologies, including next-generation wireless systems, new low-cost appliances, and innovative application and system software. (Despite ongoing discussions with the national communica-

Boys log on at a typical SARI telekiosk, or *chiraag,* which means "something that brings light" in Hindi.

tions authorities, circuit-switched voice services have not yet been offered.) Social and economic research, monitoring, and assessments begun under the Madurai pilot will also continue. ◐

▶

for only $0.40, treatment advice by e-mail.

Most farmers have little access to veterinary advice other than through unlicensed practitioners who often charge exorbitant rates for questionable diagnoses. Direct access to experts at the Tamil Nadu Veterinary Sciences University has provided villagers with cures for various animal ailments without having to leave their village.

In Attapati village, Priya sent a photo of her limping chicken to the veterinary college. The disease was identified as curled-toe paralysis which is caused by Vitamin-B deficiency. The medication was communicated online for a cost of only $0.40 versus $4 earlier.

SARI has partnered with Aravind Eye Hospital to provide online eye consultations. Kiosk operators are trained take pictures of

eyes and then e-mail them to hospital doctors. Based on these images, doctors can make a preliminary diagnosis and recommend various courses of action: to make an appointment, try a home remedy, visit a local eye clinic, or undergo an operation.

Using an online questionnaire, villagers themselves can send digital pictures of their eyes. Diagnoses are e-mailed back to them, and appointments for treatment are made as needed. About 80 patients have used this service in a six-month period.

In addition to screening movies, the telekiosks also provide offline services such as photography (e.g., for passports) and test training including sample questions and lectures. SARI wants to collaborate with ICICI to provide online banking facilities to villagers and possibly a low-cost ATM. ◐

ADAPTIVE TECHNOLOGIES

Off the map

▶DakNet, Karnataka State, India

WIRELESS BROADBAND CAN HAVE THE biggest impact in rural areas where there is the least infrastructure. In these poor areas, with limited or unavailable connectivity options, a little bit of wireless can go a long way.

First Mile Solutions, based in Cambridge, Massachusetts, has been working to develop an affordable, low-risk wireless infrastructure to bridge the digital divide and jumpstart the rural communications market.

"We don't really know how people are going to use infrastructure where it hasn't existed," says Founder and Managing Partner Amir Alexander Hasson. "It may not even make sense yet to call it a market, the some 4 billion people living in rural areas who lack communications infrastructure."

In collaboration with Professors Sandy Pentland and Rich Fletcher of MIT Media Lab, Hasson has developed a "store-and-forward" infrastructure for rural areas using local transportation. Villages surrounding a town within 10 to 80 kilometers have an array of transportation

vehicles passing through on a daily basis, raising a promising connectivity possibility. In addition to picking up and dropping off passengers, what if you could do the same with data?

Originally funded and patented by the MIT Media Lab, DakNet—the name comes from the Hindi word "dak," which means "post" or "postal"—has been implemented in India and Cambodia (and soon Nigeria). DakNet is essentially a store-and-forward wireless broadband network using a Mobile Access Point, or MAP, device that is mounted on any vehicle that frequently passes by a series of villages.

When the vehicle comes in range of a Wi-Fi-enabled kiosk within the village (up to 1 km depending on line-of-sight, velocity, and use of antennas), the MAP automatically senses a wireless connection with a kiosk and delivers and collects data at an average "goodput" (adjusted for connection-dropping) of 2.3 Mbps. After making a routine circuit, the vehicle returns to a hub, such as a cyber café, VSAT, or post office, and uplinks to the

---

THINGS TO REMEMBER

▶ Applications that are compatible in different settings increase the chances of their adoption. In India, DakNet worked as an intranet for land record changes. In Cambodia, it is used for e-mail and as a non-real-time search engine.

▶ A project will run smoothly when every part of the value chain has a buy-in to the project; that is, state government, bus driver, end user, and so on.

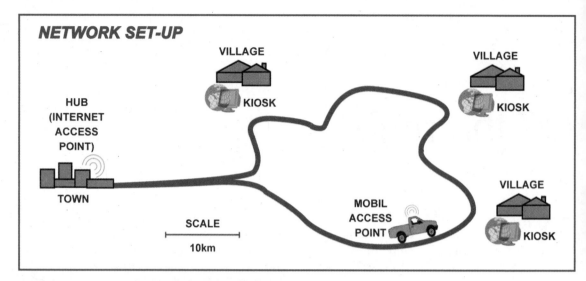

NETWORK SET-UP

VILLAGE

KIOSK

VILLAGE

KIOSK

HUB
(INTERNET
ACCESS
POINT)

TOWN

VILLAGE

KIOSK

MOBIL
ACCESS
POINT

SCALE

10km

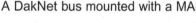

A DakNet bus mounted with a MAP.

A DakNet hub with satellite uplink.

Internet backbone.

The result is broadband intranet wireless access and applications to areas where there may even be no telephone, for under $500 per village.

Initial installations of DakNet are done by the First Mile Solution team, which also builds human-resource development capacity by training local teams about wireless networking, empowering them to maintain, expand, and upgrade the network themselves.

Although the data transport provided by DakNet is not real-time, a very large amount of data can be moved at once, supporting a wide variety of non-real time applications, including audio and video messaging, e-mail, community bulletin boards, public health announcements, and music and video broadcasts. Information-intensive applications include collection of environmental sensor information, voting, census/polling, health records, and land records; as well as Web services such as searching and browsing, e-commerce, and voice-mail over IP. The service can also track the movement of goods. ◉

Store-and-forward stepping-stones

IN KARNATAKA STATE, THE LOCAL GOVERNment has pioneered the computerization of land records in what is recognized as the first state-level e-governance initiative in India. The Bhoomi project has been successfully implemented at district headquarters across Karnataka to completely replace the physical land-records system.

DakNet has taken Bhoomi one step farther, however, by decentralizing the land-records database to villages up to 70 km from the district headquarters, or "taluka," in Doddaballapur. DakNet uses a public government bus with a Mobile Access Point, or MAP, to transport land-record requests from each village kiosk back to the taluka server. The server processes requests and outputs land records that are then delivered back to the kiosks for printing and payment (about $0.32 per land record).

Amir Hasson answered questions about DakNet's design and economics and about a second implementation in Cambodia that delivers Internet access to remote schools through a similar store-and-forward wireless method.

Q. What did the Karnataka drivers think about having an antenna mounted on their buses?

A. All of the bus drivers wanted to be the first DakNet-enabled bus, but gradually they realized that if all these people were doing land records from the village, they would not be riding the bus as often, and that meant they will lose revenue. At that point, they could not really object because they had orders from Karnataka's revenue department and e-governance department. Nevertheless, to scale the network, you would need to provide the right incentives for the means of transport as well.

Q. Does DakNet have a business model

associated with Bhoomi?

A. The Bhoomi project really is not designed to make money. It is going to take about 6.5-7 years for the total investment in those kiosks to pay off if they are doing only land records for Rs.15 per record. Other services need to be provided or we might need to develop cheap machines that just do land records very cheaply.

Q. Did you develop software for the project?

A. We worked with the National Informatic Center and customized their front end to work with our system. So it uses the same database (backend) but a different front end that works in a store-and-forward or asynchronous mode.

In India, we just provided an intranet—the bus going back and forth taking land records—but in Cambodia, we are actually providing Internet access. You have full-fledged e-mail accounts using Outlook Express on each of the computers. People have e-mail IDs, and they are globally connected. With a non-real-time search engine, they can also enter a keyword search, such as "malaria," and the search is sent to our server in Cambridge where the cached results are e-mailed back to the user who can then browse the results offline.

Q. What is the business model in Cambodia?

A. It is much more of a long-term approach where the schools have been funded by the World Bank and other donors as community centers of excellence with some minimal tuition. But as the schools have an economic development dynamic within their premises, they may become a commercial center that the villagers use for their daily needs.

Q. Do you see the store-and-forward

▶

▶

design as a long-term solution? Is this a stepping-stone or the end point?

A. Communications is a fundamental right and there are many advantages to real-time connectivity at some point. But what we are arguing is that you need a way to get there, and DakNet is a stepping-stone that's designed to be more or less seamless. We would like to position ourselves as a provider of seed technology that can also grow to provide the technology that is demanded as each village develops.

A. What are some of the advantages of the store-and-forward design over a cell phone?

A. There are a lot of disadvantages of providing a real-time network especially if you're working in a shared-access kind of model. If you have a telecenter, with one phone booth for the whole village, the catch there is that the person who is being called is almost never at that phone booth. Someone has to record the message for the person who was called and then deliver the message. If you are paying for that kind of infrastructure, you need to provide access devices (phone/computer/handheld) in households and not as a shared model. The private sector will perk up when people will start to be able to afford their own access devices and we start to move away from the shared model. That's a kind of gold mine here. ◑

Beyond 'off the shelf'

▶Jhai Remote IT Village Project, Vientiane, Laos

LIFE IS HARD IN THE VILLAGES 85 KM NORTH OF Vientiane, in rural Laos. Each year brings torrential rains followed by high temperatures and a thick red dust. The people here are deprived of telephone connections and power and have limited access to cellular services because of the surrounding mountain range.

But the Jhai Foundation in San Francisco has been busy here introducing techniques to farmers to help them grow surpluses of rice and other crops. The foundation has shown expert women weavers how to use natural dyes to weave textiles for export. To profit from surpluses, however, the farmers need accurate and timely information about pricing in the market town of Phon Hong and in Vientiane. And the women must communicate with emigrant Laotians to increase the rate of return from the sale of their woven goods.

After researching alternatives like expensive radiotelephones and impractical fiber line, Jhai Foundation's Remote Village IT program found a sustainable, low-cost solution for the villagers through the combination of a low-power computer, wireless broadband, and voice-over IP.

Overcoming the lack of a power supply and conditions unfriendly to off-the-shelf technologies, Jhai's team of engineers, led by personal computer pioneer Lee Felsenstein, developed a 12-watt computer prototype that can withstand dumping in a bucket of water, battering by dust storms, and a fall from the table. The team located an Indian-manufactured, bicycle-pedaled generator to supply power. (Because of the monsoon season, solar panels were too inefficient.) The bicycle cost is only one third of a solar-powered set-up. One minute of pedaling generates about five minutes of power.

The computer connects wirelessly to an antenna on the roof, which sends a signal to a nearby

---

THINGS TO REMEMBER

▶Because off-the-shelf equipment can't always withstand harsh field conditions, practitioners should determine whether they will need to research and develop special hardware, including alternative power sources.

▶Where knowledge of English is low, local-language applications may be critical. When local scripts are not available and/or literacy is low, voice applications may be an appropriate substitute.

▶Involving end users in each stage of the project creates a sense of personal ownership and can smooth adoption of the technology.

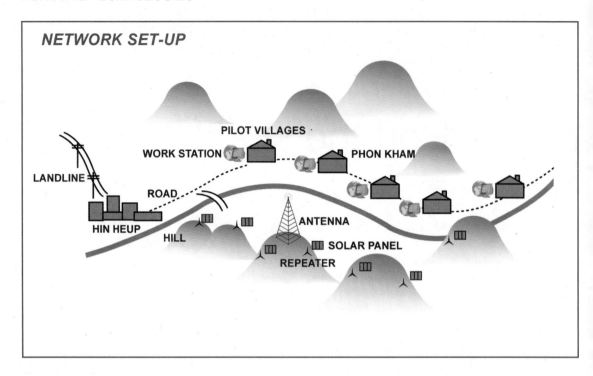

NETWORK SET-UP

PILOT VILLAGES

WORK STATION

PHON KHAM

LANDLINE

ROAD

HIN HEUP

HILL

ANTENNA

SOLAR PANEL

REPEATER

mountain, which is then forwarded 25 km to Phon Hong, the closest town with phone lines. A wireless LAN centered at the mountaintop relay station will eventually transmit signals between five villages and a server at Phon Hong Hospital, enabling access to the Internet over the Lao telephone system.

The computer will run a Laotian version of the Linux-based graphical desktop KDE, which was developed by a student-teacher team at the National University of Laos in Vientiane under the direction of former IBM software developer Anousak Souphavanh. The suite of business tools allows Laotians to browse the Web, send e-mail, and create simple documents.

Lee Thorn, Chairman and Founder of the Jhai Foundation, calls the localization into Laotian "probably the hardest part of the whole project." To generate fonts in Laotian, for example, the team had to create its own Unicode, a standard for encoding letters and other characters in any language. The entire system was built with the needs

of villagers closely in mind. They were involved in every stage of the project from the very beginning. Minimal use of outside "experts" has encouraged local ownership of the project.

This network will enable villagers to make telephone calls within Laos and internationally using voice-over IP. It will also enable the accounting, letter writing, and e-mail that are so important for the villagers' start-up enterprises.

In addition to incubating the business aspirations of local farmers, builders, and weavers, the set-up will facilitate communication with distant family members who send remittances and who are potential business partners with the villagers. The community will also be able to effectively communicate with other organizations like the Jhai Foundation and seek development help on its own terms.

"We're building the system to last for years, a whole social, technical, and economic tool that looks like a system and is owned by poor people," Thorn says. "The Lao members of the team, including the villagers, see this effort as a gift from

A Jhai team member at the "Wi-Fi Tree."

A bicycle-powered computer in Vientiane.

A Lao-enabled browser.

the people of Laos to the world's rural poor. A sustainable, replicable solution."

While monsoons and road washouts have caused some delays, testing of the Phon Kham village link to the Internet began in early 2003. Using a laptop, Vorasone Dengkayaphichith, Jhai's country coordinator, sent e-mail and pictures, and, on January 23rd, used VoIP to speak to colleagues in Canada, the United States, Sweden, and Laos. The signal went from Phon Kham village via a station in a tree on a hill (2.4 km) to a water tower in Phon Hong (9 km) and then to the Internet via a phone line. Software problems foiled a first attempt to install in February, and the team plans to return to Laos in November 2003 to implement this project.

Although the Jhai project north of Vientiane still faces certain logistical issues, it has received inquires from India, Indonesia, and many other countries where telecommunications and power distribution remain limited. The project team plans to refine the Jhai approach for use in other locations. ◐

Solid state

Jhai Foundation's Remote Village IT program found a sustainable, low-cost solution for villagers with its own durable, theft-resistant computer. The Jhai Computer, with an MZ-104 CPU board, 64 MB of RAM, and a 96 MB disk-on-chip, is designed to withstand harsh conditions, including dust, dirt, water, and humidity.

REBUILDING NATIONS

Wi-Fi Wild West

▶Internet Project Kosovo, Pristina, Kosovo

INTERNET PROJECT KOSOVO, OR IPKO, launched wireless broadband connectivity in Kosovo on September 20, 1999, in the weeks after the war, as a project of the International Rescue Committee (IRC). NATO bombing had destroyed much of Kosovo's communications infrastructure. The Serbs who ran it were gone.

At the time, UN and Humanitarian Agencies had no effective way of communicating or sharing information, and they were clamoring for connectivity. Most were using expensive satellite-based communications, and the default was for each to deploy its own solution. But this was expensive and duplicative and did not connect the local community. IPKO's alternative was to install one satellite dish and build an 802.11 wireless local loop network around it.

The deployment kicked off with a $175,000 loan from IRC and a 3.8-mm satellite dish donated by Interpacket Networks. The team installed the dish and an 802.11b wireless network in Pristina. IPKO sold service to every UN agency, NATO, international NGOs, Internet cafés, and businesses. It provided free connectivity to schools, hospitals, the university, and local NGOs.

"We were in a rather blessedly unregulated environment," remembers IPKO cofounder Paul Meyer. "Our license was a half-page M.O.U. with the UN. That served as our operating license for three and a half years until finally the government passed a telecom law. So I can sing the virtues of free regulation. It really was the Wild West."

After six months, IPKO was incorporated as a local NGO. In the course of its first year, it began expanding to other main urban centers in Kosovo. Nine months after inception, it launched a dial-up service. After a year of operation, it opened the IPKO Institute of Technology, a technology train-

---

THINGS TO REMEMBER

▶Initial financial support is critical. The funding can be a donation, a financial loan, or loan of equipment.

▶Open regulatory environments and zero bureaucratic hassles expedite the deployment of wireless technologies.

▶Connectivity for its own sake will not ensure project adoption. Look beyond the technology and develop applications to meet the needs of local users.

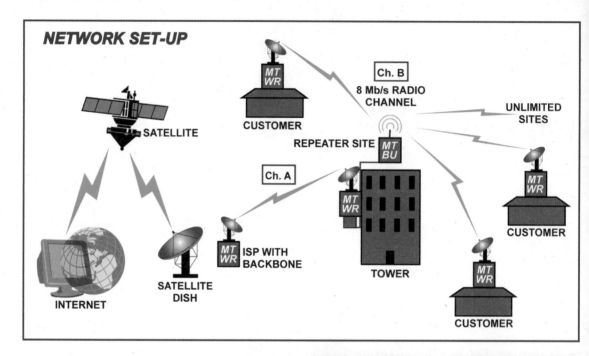

NETWORK SET-UP

SATELLITE

CUSTOMER

Ch. B
8 Mb/s RADIO
CHANNEL

UNLIMITED
SITES

REPEATER SITE

Ch. A

ISP WITH
BACKBONE

TOWER

CUSTOMER

CUSTOMER

INTERNET

SATELLITE
DISH

ing institute in Pristina that now provides CISCO, Microsoft, and other training courses to more than 200 students at a time.

"IPKO was founded to provide the tools, knowledge, and environment required for Kosovo to participate in the global information society," Meyer says. "It has done so."

In late 2000, its Internet-service-provider business was spun off as a for-profit subsidiary (IPKONet) owned by the nonprofit Institute and its employees. IPKONet now has a nationwide 155-MB wireless backbone, a wireless link across Albania to the fiber-optic backbone in the Adriatic Sea, Wi-Fi networks in the main cities of Kosovo, and national dial-up access. It is the leading Internet provider and one of the largest businesses in Kosovo.

IPKO was profitable from the outset, and its start-up loan was repaid in four months. In the years since its founding, it has raised commercial bank debt to finance network upgrades and expansion.

IPKO attributes much of its success to Kosovo's permissive regulatory environment and the critical

An IPKO dish in Pristina.

mass of organization customers. Both the satellite dish donation and a working capital loan were crucial to kicking off, while a commitment to hand over the system met with good hands in well-trained Kosovar managers and technicians. Today, Meyer recommends relying on local infrastructure and local operators where they exist, providing access to the community and civil society, and committing to leaving the system behind. ◑

Applications are harder than networks

At the "Wireless Internet Opportunity for Developing Countries" conference at UN Headquarters on June 26, 2003, Paul Meyer, Co-Founder of Internet Project Kosovo and CEO of Voxiva, urged the development community deploying ICTs to "focus on the information flow problems you're trying to solve, not on the technology."

"*I think that International development agencies have spent too much time thinking about technologies and networks and not enough time thinking about information flow problems. Technology is not an end in itself. It is only valuable if it facilitates flows of key information and addresses critical problems. Start with the fundamental problem: What information needs to flow where? Then figure out how to put together existing technologies, networks, and applications to solve it.*

"*Connectivity is not enough. The potential of information technology is not realized when kids can chat and download music videos at Internet cafés in the developing world. The potential is realized when people at the periphery can participate meaningfully in the broader world; when businesses can transact seamlessly with one another; when governments can make decisions informed by accurate, timely information and provide critical services to their citizens.*

"*There are three lessons I've taken from my experience at IPKO in Kosovo and at Voxiva, the company I now run.*

"*First, international-development agencies should not be telecom companies. They should work with and become customers of existing providers. At IPKO in Kosovo, we built a national wireless backbone because we had to. There was no existing infrastructure. Luckily, most countries in the world have existing and rapidly expanding telecom, mobile phone, and Internet networks. Go to the far corners of Uganda, and*

there's mobile telephony. Companies like MTN in Uganda and IPKO in Kosovo are building out infrastructure. International development agencies and policy makers should focus on the policy problems, the information flow, and the applications and solutions that are required to promote health or education, for example. That focus on applications does much more good in promoting access because it creates a market and demand for connectivity. By focusing on the policy problems they are chartered to solve, international development institutions can be aggregators of demand for connectivity.

"*The second lesson I've learned is that applications are harder than infrastructure. Figuring out what key pieces of information need to flow where is hard work. For example, designing and implementing a decision support and communication application for a Ministry of Health to track disease outbreaks requires deep understanding of the work processes of the doctors and administrators at every level. Furthermore, introducing a system of real-time information necessarily changes the way an organization functions, making change management and training keys to success. People who are experts in health or education or microfinance should focus their energies on figuring out how those sectors can benefit from real-time information flows. They shouldn't spend their time worrying about connectivity.*

"*The final lesson I've learned is that there are a lot more phones in the world than computers. Moreover, phones don't require literacy. If the developing world is to benefit from applications that address information flow problems in key sectors like health and education, we need to look beyond just the Internet and PCs. If applications can be extended to every computer and every phone in the developing world, then we will have the reach to make a real difference in solving critical problems there.*"◑

Picking up the PCs

▶**UN Development Program, Kabul, Afghanistan**

Today, only 6 percent of the population of Afghanistan has access to electricity. Many Afghans have never made a phone call, let alone sent e-mail or surfed the Internet. The nation is arguably at the far end—the bottom end—of the digital divide.

But the UN Development Program in Afghanistan is working to change this, at least for a small but growing percentage of Kabul's 2.5 million residents, thanks to a $300,000 grant from France, a wireless LAN, and new telekiosks at the airport and in post offices less than 10 km from the Ministry of Communications.

Four of the telekiosks, which include five PCs and a printer, were opened on July 6, 2003. Two were linked to the Ministry with fiber, and, by mid-August, two were connected wirelessly to base stations at the Ministry. Each post-office telekiosk costs $19,500 to set up. If revenue predictions are correct, each is expected to generate up to $30 per day from local users.

In the first month, the initial four telekiosks received 2,600 customer visits. In the second month, with six telekiosks in operation, there were 2,410 customer visits. The number dropped because of power-supply problems and because two of the six telekiosks were only open for half a month. UNDP reports that all nine telekiosks were functioning by late September.

Two "animators" at each telekiosk help Afghans learn basic computer and Internet skills. While most users are male, an outreach effort is under way to bring in more women and girls. The telekiosks should enable schoolteachers and children, government employees, health workers, and others in Kabul to do e-mail and access the Internet. A Web site will support both Dari and English and eventually Pashto.

The majority of the people visiting the telekiosks are first-time users and need basic computer training. "We had anticipated that most people visiting the telekiosks would be returning

---

THINGS TO REMEMBER

▶In a nation or region recovering from war or crisis, wireless networks can serve as a fast substitute for national telecom infrastructure, especially where there are few regulatory barriers.

▶Making use of existing solid structures for shared Internet access can reduce the cost of deployment.

▶Sporadic availability of power can shut down operations, causing revenue losses.

Most telekiosk users in Kabul have been male, but UNDP is reaching out to women and girls.

refugees from places where they received computer training or workers at international organizations that would want to use the Internet," says Rafiqullah Kakar, the National Project Coordinator for UNDP-Afghanistan. "But most users were first-time users of technology." A fee for training may be added; $.20 -.40 per hour at one telekiosk could generate another $5 to $10 per day.

In Kabul, infrastructure is still limited, so UNDP's decision to link the telekiosks with a wireless LAN was made early. "It was a cost-effective way to provide a quick and easy connection to the Ministry's satellite Internet backbone access while avoiding any infrastructure problems that may face a landline implementation," reports Karen Gray, a project consultant to UNDP, in a memorandum.

The benefits of wireless LAN outnumber the inconvenience of installing masts up to 120 feet tall in some locations. The WLAN is high bandwidth and quick and easy to install. It faces no

regulatory issues, can be self-managed, and can link to the Ministry's 1.5 Mbps satellite Internet backbone.

Three base stations were installed at the Ministry to give 360-degree coverage of the city within a range of 10 km. The amplifier has 250 mw of transmit power. The farthest telekiosk from the Ministry is 8 km. Each base station unit can support 64 sites (total 194 sites) because each is set to a different channel (within the allowed frequency band). Currently, there is only sufficient bandwidth on the satellite data access backbone to support 20 sites.

As the UNDP telekiosks are expanded to Afghanistan's other provinces, the network design will need to be revised. Some provinces have one to five post offices in the main city. The more rural provinces have one post office in the main city and others spread as much as 50 to 100 km from the main post office.

A specific technology goal for the deployment is to determine whether a wireless LAN really is fea-

Avid newcomers to the Web.

Kabul's airport telekiosk.

sible in such a challenging environment. To encourage sustainability, UNDP has committed to providing hands-on and classroom training on wireless networking to Ministry employees involved in the project. ◖◗

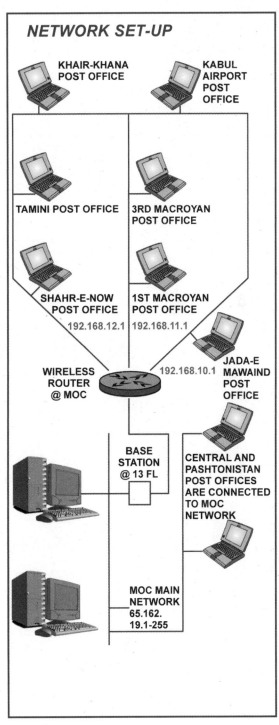

NETWORK SET-UP

GUIDELINES TO COUNTRIES

Proposed Guidelines in Support of Local Experimentation and Early Deployment of Broadband Wireless Internet

Prepared by the Secretariat of the United Nations ICT Task Force and the Wireless Internet Institute on the basis of discussions at the "Wireless Internet Opportunity for Developing Countries" conference at United Nations Headquarters in New York City on June 26, 2003.

WIRELESS INTERNET TECHNOLOGIES AND applications are in their early developmental stages, and their potential economic and social benefits appear to be considerable especially in the context of the United Nations Millennium Development Goals. International development experts and leading IT corporations consider wireless Internet technologies essential to bridging the digital divide in developing countries at a manageable cost and within a reasonable timeframe.

These new technologies and applications, however, are emerging in many different situations, often outside the operational landscape of traditional telecommunications services, and with new types of participants from both the private and public sectors. Wireless Internet applications resulting from grassroots initiatives may be seen as disruptive and can hit unintended roadblocks in the form of local regulations and lack of understanding of their potential. Conversely, proper government support and incentives can accelerate their successful implementation at little cost and with significant immediate economic and social benefits for the poor.

Each country presents unique characteristics and conditions with respect to wireless Internet deployment, from a geographic, social, economic, regulatory, and telecommunications infrastructure standpoint. There are, however, several regulatory and economic success factors that country authorities should consider. To facilitate such local review, the following guidelines to governments wanting to support the experimentation and early deployment of wireless Internet infrastructure applications, are proposed.

1. Identify, promote, and establish national consensus on the potential benefits of wireless Internet applications and local priorities.

A key factor of success for wireless Internet deployment is a generally supportive environment, a prerequisite of which is adequate awareness of policy makers, the public and private sectors, and the local media.

United Nations Millennium Development Goal No. 8, Target 18, states: "In cooperation with the private sector, make available the benefits of new technologies, especially information and communications." There is a general agreement that

Internet access is a key success factor in making these new technologies work for development. In many geographic areas, however, the cost of expanding Internet connectivity with landlines or cable remains prohibitive for the foreseeable future, while available bandwidth is increasing exponentially in developed countries, furthering the digital divide.

Raising awareness and building national consensus about the benefits of low-cost broadband wireless Internet infrastructure solutions is therefore an important first step.

One complex challenge is to clearly differentiate the broadband capabilities of IEEE 802.xx-based technologies for fixed infrastructure from the low-bandwidth mobile solutions offered by current cellular telephony and personal-devices networks.

Local governments may also inventory those applications that may contribute the most to bridging the digital divide both from a geographic and social standpoint, and foster economic development, job creation, and productivity gains in all economic sectors. Of particular interest for developing countries are opportunities in the 3 "e's": e-government, e-education, e-health (a fourth, e-commerce, is sometimes also included); rural-areas coverage, small business connectivity, the development of local ICT services including private-sector ISPs and voice-over IP services.

Identifying leading applications, which may drive the initial use of wireless Internet infrastructure and distribution, will further develop support for wireless Internet solutions among key constituents.

2. Adopt minimum regulations supporting the use of unlicensed spectrum and ICT industry standards.

A second critical success factor is the leverage of internationally recognized norms. Harmonization creates significant economies of scale for equipment manufacturers, software developers, and off-the-shelf solutions. It is therefore in the best interest of countries to closely follow and support the norms and recommendations of the following organizations:

▶ For spectrum policy and standards references:
　▶ Institute of Electrical and Electronics Engineers (IEEE)
　　▶ ITU World Radiocommunication Conference
▶ For manufacturers standards compliance, interoperability, and quality assurance:
　▶ Wi-Fi Alliance for 802.11 products
　▶ WiMax Forum for 802.16 products

The single-most important step to support wireless Internet applications is to develop a spectrum policy that allocates bands for unlicensed applications, such as the 2.4- and 5-GHz bands currently unlicensed in a number of countries.

In a first step toward worldwide spectrum allocation to wireless Internet applications, the ITU in its July 4, 2003 World Radio Conference communiqué indicates that it "successfully established new frequency allocations to the mobile service in the bands 5150-5350 MHz and 5470-5725 MHz for the implementation of wireless access systems including RLANs. Wireless devices that do not require individual licenses are being used to create broadband networks in homes, offices, and schools. These networks are also used in public facilities in so-called hotspots such as airports, cafes, hotels, hospitals, train stations, and conference sites to offer broadband access to the Internet....

"The lower part of the 5-GHz spectrum will be predominantly used for indoor applications with the first 100 MHz (5150-5250 MHz) restricted to indoor use. The use of these frequency bands is conditional to provisions that provide for interference mitigation mechanisms and power-emission limits to avoid interference into other radio communication services operating in the same spectrum range."

Each country may have existing spectrum allocations that need to be adjusted. A close monitoring of international regulatory activities and the adaptation of local spectrum policies is therefore recommended.

3. Update telecommunications regulations to foster market opportunities, optimize existing infrastructure resources, and free competition

among wireless Internet service providers.

Although situations will vary greatly from one country to another, four areas need careful attention from a telecommunication regulatory perspective:

(*a*) Access to an Internet backbone is a prerequisite for successful deployment of broadband wireless Internet services. *To the extent possible, telecommunications regulations regime should foster a competitive Internet backbone market.* Private- or public-sector entities outside the telecommunications industry should be allowed to contribute their backbone capacity. This is particularly important in regions with underused backbone capacity. As an example, GrameenPhone in Bangladesh was made possible by the collaboration of the National Railway System contributing access to its fiber-optic network. Conversely, if only a few backbone service providers exist, they should be obligated to open up their infrastructure to independent service providers.

(*b*) If no backbone is available, alternative solutions include broadband terrestrial wireless links, satellite stations and power grids. *Appropriate incentives encouraging such solutions should be implemented.*

(*c*) At the final distribution level, *Internet service providers, or ISPs, implementing wireless Internet solutions need to be facilitated by telecommunications regulations and operate in the context of free market competition.*

(*d*) Legacy regulations concerning radio communications, some related to law-enforcement agencies or the military, can also create unintended obstacles for wireless Internet ISPs including for the physical deployment of antennas and radio-communications equipment. These should be adapted to the specific needs of wireless ISPs as in such landmark cooperation agreements facilitated by the regulator between the private sector and the NTIA (National Telecommunications and Information Administration) on use of unlicensed spectrum in the United States (see Appendix 1 on p. 103).

4. Identify key available resources and foster cooperation among potential actors.

Wireless Internet infrastructure and services can leverage a number of existing resources in any given country:

▶ backbone operators and owners of fiber-optic networks including governments, private-sector networks, telcos, power-grid operators, and satellite communications operators;

▶ owners of real estate and high points with adequate power supply and security to install antennas, such as existing radio communications towers or possibly public-sector buildings such as post offices or other types of standard venues;

▶ systems integrators with the technical capabilities to install and maintain wireless equipment such as towers, cabling, hub-integrated antennas, wireless modems, control and network management systems, routers, cables, uninterruptible power supplies, racks, etc.;

▶ operators of similar services such as TV broadcasting, cellular telephony, computer maintenance organizations, and power distribution;

▶ financial-sector interested to fund start-up ISPs;

▶ community leaders eager to provide Internet access to their constituents;

▶ incumbent telecommunications operators; and

▶ providers of know-how and training services.

It is recommended to support venues such as conferences or seminars on wireless Internet to increase awareness and initiate dialogues and cooperation among key decision makers from both the private and public sectors.

5. Support the experimentation of new services and encourage the aggregation of demand for bandwidth.

Although wireless Internet initiatives can be perceived as disruptive and infringing on existing regulations, they are an important source of information to adapt regulations and develop public-sector strategies. *Governments are encouraged to support early initiatives with interim measures until appropriate regulatory adjustments are made.*

One of the most important factors of success for wireless ISPs is a rapid increase of initial demand for connectivity, which allows for a faster break-even on operating expenses. This can be achieved through initial aggregation of demand based on applications for local public services such as schools, universities, health services, and public administration. Business, agriculture, and private uses will inevitably add to the mix once service is available. In very underserved areas, it is likely that initial viable aggregation will occur through the deployment of wireless Internet kiosks operated by small entrepreneurs.

Governments are encouraged to deploy applications in the area of e-government, e-education, and e-health to leverage the use of Internet access by the general public. Governments should also encourage local public services to use the infrastructure of local wireless ISPs.

6. Follow-up and support of wireless Internet developments at governmental and intergovernmental levels, including sharing of best practices.

It is anticipated that wireless Internet technologies and applications will continue to evolve rapidly, which makes it important for *governments and private-sector leaders to remain abreast of other countries' experiences, regulatory work at the international level, best practices, and latest innovations.* ◍

National Telecommunications and Information Administration
For Immediate Release
January 31, 2003

Contact: Clyde Ensslin or Ranjit de Silva, 202-482-7002

AGREEMENT REACHED REGARDING U.S. POSITION ON 5-GHz WIRELESS ACCESS DEVICES

Executive Branch agencies of the U.S. government, in cooperation with the Federal Communications Commission (FCC) and industry proponents of 5 GHz Wireless Access System (WAS) devices, have reached agreement on modifications to the U.S. position with respect to these devices, for use in international fora.

"I am very pleased that the participants from the federal government and the private sector have come to a consensus that satisfies both of their interests," said Assistant Secretary of Commerce and NTIA Administrator Nancy J. Victory. "In achieving this, the Bush Administration has continued its goal of stimulating the economy and ensuring the national defense and preserving the leadership of the U.S. high-tech sector. Based on these changes, the U.S. is now able to formalize its position with respect to earth exploration satellite systems, mobile, and radiolocation services at 5 GHz and will now fully support these allocations," Victory said.

The NTIA, FCC, NASA and Department of Defense (DoD), working closely with industry in detailed technical meetings, have agreed to modify the required Dynamic Frequency Selection (a listen-before-transmit mechanism) detection threshold characteristics contained in the U.S. proposal for WRC-03 Agenda Item 1.5 as follows:

A. The Threshold value is modified from -67 dBm to -64 dBm for 1W to 200 mW devices and -62 dBm for < 200 mW devices. This would now apply to the 5250-5350 MHz and 5470-5725 MHz bands.

B. The U.S. position of only allocating the 5150-5350 MHz band to the mobile service will be modified to include an allocation to the mobile service in the 5470-5725 MHz band and the resolution for continued studies on this band will be deleted.

C. As a consequence, of these modifications, the U.S. position on the Earth Exploration Satellite Service allocation at 5460-5570 MHz will be to support this allocation.

The changes to the U.S. position will now allow the U.S. to seek a mobile allocation at the International Telecommunication Union (ITU) World Radiocommunication Conference in Geneva in June and July 2003 in both bands sought by industry (5150-5350 MHz and 5470-5725 MHz) while ensuring protection of vital DoD radars.

The previous technical requirements for these systems, which must include DFS, have also been modified based on new information recently explored. These changes not only continue to ensure that the vital DoD radars are protected, but ease sharing conditions for the WAS systems.

VENDOR RESOURCES

Understanding the wireless Internet value chain*

By Amir Alexander Hasson

THE IEEE 802.11- AND 802.16-BASED WIRELESS networking technologies—collectively, the wireless Internet—have emerged as a digital-communications standard over the past four years, producing a dynamic value chain of suppliers, vendors, and consumers. The technology's affordability, ease of setup, standardization, and favorable regulatory environment in target markets have enabled rapid development, with some clear cost and performance advantages over wire-line networking (i.e., Ethernet) for homes and offices. It has reduced total cost of ownership for networking and served as a high-performance medium to distribute available bandwidth.

Although the market for wireless Internet technologies has become saturated in some areas and failed to meet some bullish industry projections, it has been one of the only large growth areas within the IT and telecommunications sectors during the recent economic slump, and many strategists consider it a disruptive technology.

The wireless Internet value chain is comprised of three broad segments, beginning with network equipment manufacturers, network software and application providers, and network integrators and operators (see Figure 1).

Equipment manufacturers produce the basic networking components that constitute the physi-cal layer of any wireless network. As network equipment developed, so did the need for tools to manage, operate, and protect wireless networks, which led to several new companies entering the value chain as application and software providers.

The variety of these tools, combined with the increasing demand for wireless networks in public and enterprise IT markets, led to an increasing need for packaged solutions, spawning another group of new entrants (and new divisions within consulting companies) known as system integra-tors. Once a critical installed base of wireless Internet-enabled devices and users was estab-lished, new market opportunities to capitalize on and operate wireless networks as an Internet access service emerged. This led to the widespread proliferation of public and private wireless Internet-enabled networks throughout the United States, Europe, and parts of Asia-Pacific.

The equipment manufacturer segment of the value chain consists of chipset makers, access point and client radio producers, antenna and amplifier vendors, and producers of wireless-enabled access devices (Figure 2).

Chipset makers create the core wireless technol-ogy radios and firmware (software that enables wireless networking to work with operating sys-tems and other hardware components). These chipsets are then integrated into wireless hardware

Figure 1: An overview of the wireless Internet value chain.

| Wireless Internet Equipment Manufacturers | → | Wireless Internet Application and Software Providers | → | Wireless Internet Integrators and Operators | → | END USERS |

*The listings in this chapter are not meant to be exhaustive but indicative of available resources in each of the categories.

Figure 2: The wireless networking equipment segment.

Wireless Chipsets		Access Points and Client Radios		2.4/5.3 Ghz Antennas and Amplifiers		Wireless-Enabled Access Devices
Proxim	→	Alvarion	→	Hyperlink Tech.	→	Dell
Intersil		Nomadix		Cushcraft		IBM
Agere		ValuePoint		Buffalo		HP-Compaq
Aironet (Cisco)		Linksys (Cisco)		Hughes		Motorola
Intel		D-Link		Luxul Corp.		Toshiba
Atheros		Proxim		Pacific Wireless		Nokia
Texas Instrument		Symbol		Fractus		Siemens
Broadcom		SMC		Motia		Palm
		3COM		Vivato		Sony
		NetGear				
		Motorola				
		Firetide				
		Lucent				
		Alcatel				
		Siemens				
		Hughes				

products such as client radio cards (used for laptops and PDAs) and access points, which connect client radios to an available backbone such as DSL. Other companies focus on producing antennas and amplifiers required to connect wireless clients with access points over long distances or in unfavorable networking environments (802.16 technology). As the demand for wireless networking products has grown, manufacturers of PCs, PDAs, and even cell phones have also begun to introduce 802.11-compliant wireless chipsets into their products. This segment of equipment manufacturers has seen tremendous growth in recent years and has been the primary winner within the overall wireless Internet value chain.

The application and software provider segment consists of providers for network security; network optimization; network management; and integra-

tion with back-end systems for accounting, billing, and customer-relationship management (Figure 3).

One of the caveats of wireless networks has been their vulnerability to hackers, prompting a wide range of providers to develop security applications designed specifically for wireless Internet. This is perhaps the most saturated segment within the entire value chain with dozens of competing providers. Other companies have recognized a need for software that makes wireless networks (and the engineers who deploy then) "smarter," including network testing and optimization tools, advanced routing and power-management protocols, and network training programs.

Perhaps the most interesting feature within this segment, into which significant research has been invested, is "mesh networking" which aims to enable any 802.11-enabled device to also serve as a router to connect surrounding 802.11-enabled devices to the Internet indirectly through other devices that may be connected to the Internet. Another important area within this segment is net-

Amir Alexander Hasson is Founder and Managing Partner of First Mile Solutions in Cambridge, Massachusetts.

Figure 3: The wireless Internet application and software segment.

Network Security	Network Optimization	Network Management	Accounting, Billing, CRM
BlueSocket	Berkeley	Birdstep Tech	iPass
Elixar	Varitronics	Bridgewater	Billing Concepts
Escalon Networks	Systems	Systems	RockSteady
Fortress	Mesh Networks	Cirond Tech	hereUare Comm.
Technologies	Radiant Networks	NetNearU	Service Factory
Funk Software	ekahau	Airwave	Excilan
ICSA Labs	Wild Packets	SyBase	Peoplesoft
Network Chemistry	CWNP Program	WiDeFi	Nomadix
Newbury Networks	Tropos Networks		Birdstep Tech
Senforce			GRIC
Tropos			

work management software, which enables network administrators to monitor and administrate wireless networks alongside other existing networks through interfaces that capture critical variables relating to network usage and performance.

Finally there has been a particular need to develop applications that enable wireless Internet service operators to monetize network usage and tie network management software into other enterprise and legacy systems critical to business oper-

Figure 4: The wireless Internet integrators and operators segment.

Integration and Deployment	Private Hotspot Operators	Public Hotspot Operators	Industry Organizations
Concourse Comm	Hotspotzz	BAWUG (SanFran)	FierceWireless
Make 'M Wireless	iPass	NYC Wireless	WiFi Planet
BelAir Networks	T-Mobile	Consume (London)	WiFinder
First Mile Solutions	MobileStar	BC Wireless	W2I
Nortel Networks	Telia-Sonera	(Canada)	WiMAX
IBM	Wayport	Madrid Wireless	WiFi Alliance
Pronto Networks	Surf and Sip	Xnet Wireless	WECA
Wipro	WiFi Metro	(Australia)	ACM
Wavelink	SkyNetGlobal	Wireless France	IEEE
Wayport	RoomLinx	StockholmOpen.net	ITU World Radio
Alcatel	Boingo Wireless	Prenzel.net (Berlin)	Conference
Siemens	GRIC Comm	Hotel Chains	Muni Wireless
	Hotel Chains	(Marriott)	
	Restaurants	Guerilla.net	
	(Starbucks)		
	Airports (San Jose)		

ation. Many companies within this segment of the value chain are likely to be consolidated into larger IT consulting firms and system integrators because of over-saturation (Figure 4).

With the multitude of wireless networking hardware and software products on the market, entrepreneurs and larger telecom and IT consulting companies have created custom solutions to bring wireless Internet to vertical markets such as healthcare, hospitality, utilities, real estate, retail, warehousing, field service and sales, and last-mile communications. In addition to these vertical markets and home and office networking, wireless Internet has also been deployed to operate public (free) and private (commercial) networks, or "hotspots." Private hotspot operators have struggled to find a successful business model, which has caused some very ambitious operators to fail to meet expectations. This results partly from other providers (ranging from homes to restaurants with Internet connections and wireless Internet access points) offering wireless Internet access for free. As Scott Rafer, Founder of WiFinder, suggests, "wireless Internet is like air conditioning," meaning that there is a large population of consumers who have grown to expect wireless Internet access as part of a service offering. In this sense, wireless Internet access provides businesses such as hotel chains and corporate offices with reduced networking costs and a differentiation factor for marketing, but it may not yield increasing returns as a new revenue stream. The entire value chain has also been driven and reinforced by the wireless Internet industry and standards bodies that have promoted and adapted wireless technologies according to the best interest of key stakeholders.

Although parts of the wireless Internet value chain have become saturated and are undergoing consolidation, it has produced tremendous value for consumers through rapidly decreasing costs of wireless products as well as the widespread availability of wireless Internet access. The primary winners in this value chain so far have been equipment manufacturers and end users. The players and business models in the middle of the value chain are less mature and more fragmented. Although wireless Internet markets in the United States and Europe have become increasingly saturated from the supply side, there exist many opportunities for wireless Internet in emerging markets in Latin America, Asia, and Africa where there is even a greater need for affordable, distributive communications technology. ◐

Vendor directory

3COM
350 Campus Dr.
Marlborough, MA 01752-3064
Tel: 1-800-638-3266
Fax: 508-323-1111
Web: 3com.com

ACM/Assoc. Computing Machinery
1515 Broadway
New York, NY 10036
Tel: 212-626-0500
Web: acm.org

Agere
Lehigh Valley Central Campus
1110 American Parkway NE
Allentown, PA 18109
Tel: 1-800-372-2447
E-mail: docmaster@agere.com

Aironet (Cisco)
Cisco Systems, Inc.
170 West Tasman Dr.
San Jose, CA 95134
Tel: 408-526-4000
Tel: 800-553-6387
Web: cisco.com

AirWave Wireless Inc.
1700 S. El Camino Real
Ste. 500
San Mateo, CA 94402
Tel: 650-286-6100
Fax: 650-286-6101
sales@airwave.com

Alcatel
54, rue La Boétie
75008 Paris
France
Web: alcatel.com

Alvarion
International Corporate Hq.
21a HaBarzel St.
POBox 13139
Tel Aviv, 61131
Israel
Tel: 972-3-645-6262
Fax: 972-3-645-6222
E-mail: corporate-sales@alvarion.com

Atheros Communications, Inc.
529 Almanor Ave.
Sunnyvale, CA 94085-3512
Tel: 408-773-5200
Fax: 408-773-9940
info@atheros.com

BelAir Networks Inc.
603 March Rd.
Kanata, Ontario
Canada K2K 2M5
Tel: 703-736-8306
E-mail: sales@belairnetworks.com

Berkeley Varitronics Systems, Inc.
Liberty Corporate Park
255 Liberty St.
Metuchen, NJ 08840
Tel: 732-548-3737
Fax 732-548-3404
Web: bvsystems.com

Billing Concepts, Inc.
7411 John Smith Dr., Ste. 200
San Antonio, TX 78229
Tel: 888-393-5854
Fax: 210-692-0720
E-mail: sales.lec@billingconcepts.com
Web: billingconcepts.com

Birdstep Technology ASA
Bryggegata 7
N-0250 Oslo
Norway
Tel: 47-24-13-47-00
Fax: 47-24-13-47-01
E-mail: hello@birdstep.com

BlueSocket
7 New England Executive Park, 4th Flr.
Burlington, MA 01803
Toll free: 866-633-3358, Press 3
Europe: 44-0-1256-475-744
E-mail: sales@bluesocket.com

Boingo Wireless™, Inc.
1601 Cloverfield, Ste. 570
Santa Monica, CA 90404
Sales and Service: 1-800-880-4117
Fax: 1-800-880-4117
E-mail: info@boingo.com

Bridgewater Systems
303 Terry Fox Dr.
Ste. 100
Ottawa, Ontario
Canada K2K 3J1
Tel: 866-297-4636
E:mail: salesinfo@bridgewatersystems.com

Broadcom Corporation
16215 Alton Parkway
POBox 57013
Irvine, California 92619
Tel: 949-450-8700
Fax: 949-450-8710
Web: broadcom.com

Buffalo Technology (UK) Ltd
176 Buckingham Ave.
Slough, Berkshire, SL1 4RD
United Kingdom
Tel: 44-0-1753-55-50-00
Fax: 44-0-1753-53-54-20
E-mail: sales@buffalo-technology.com

Cirond Technologies
1999 South Bascom Ave.
Ste. 700
Campbell, CA 95008
Tel: 866-824-7662
E-mail: general@cirond.com

Concourse Communications
39 S. LaSalle St. Ste. 1424
Chicago, IL 60603
Tel: 312-357-2900
Fax: 312-357-2959
Web: concoursecommunications.com

Cushcraft Corporation
48 Perimeter Rd.
Manchester, NH 03103
Tel: 603-627-7877
Fax: 603-627-1764
E-mail: sales@cushcraft.com

CWNP Program
PO Box 20063
Atlanta, GA 30325
Tel: 404-305-0555.
E-mail: customercare@cwne.com

Dell
One Dell Way
Round Rock TX 78682
Tel: (512) 338-4400
Fax: (512) 728-4238
Web: dell.com

D-Link
2F, NO. 233-2 Pao-Chiao Rd.
Hsin-Tien, Taipei
Taiwan, Republic of China
Tel: 886-2-2916-1600
Fax: 886-2-2914-6299
Web: dlink.com

Ekahau, Inc.
12930 Saratoga Ave., Ste. B-9
Saratoga, CA 95070
Tel: 1-866-4EKAHAU
Fax: 1-408-725-8405
E-mail: sales@ekahau.com

Elixar, Inc
2 Davis Dr.
POBox 13169
RTP, NC 27709
Tel: 1.888.435-4927
Web: elixar.com

Escalon Networks
9229 Klemetson Dr., Ste. 200
Pleasanton, CA 94588
Tel: 925-425-9601
Fax: 925-425-9603
E-mail: info@Escalonnetworks.com

Excilan
51 Ave. de la Gare
L-1611 Luxembourg
Tel: 352-26-12-75-1
Fax: 352-26-12-75-60
Web: excilan.com

Fierce Wireless
1319 F St. NW, Ste. 604
Washington, DC 20004
Tel: 202-628-8778
Web: fiercewireless.com

Firetide, Inc.
928 Nuuanu Ave., Ste. 200
Honolulu, HI 96817
Tel: 808-528-0007
E-mail: info@firetide.com

First Mile Solutions, LLC
432 Columbia St., Ste. B13B
Cambridge, MA 02141
Tel: 617-494-1001
Fax: 616-494-6006
Web: firstmilesolutions.com

Fortress Technologies
4025 Tampa Rd., Ste. 1111
Oldsmar, FL 34677
Tel: 813-288-7388
Web: fortresstech.com

Fractus
Avda. Alcalde Barnils, 64-68
Edificio Testa-Módulo C
Sant Cugat del Vallés
08190 Barcelona (Spain)
Tel: 34-935-442-690
Fax.: 34-935-442-691
E-mail: fractus@fractus.com

Funk Software
222 Third St.
Cambridge, MA 02142
Tel: 617-497-6339/800-828-4146
Fax: 617-547-1031
E-mail: sales@funk.com

GRIC Communications, Inc
1421 McCarthy Blvd.
Milpitas, California 95035
Tel: 408-955-1920
Fax: 408-955-1968
E-mail: info@gric.com

hereUare Communications, Inc.
1600 Adams Dr.
Menlo Park, CA, 94025
Tel: 650-688-5778
Fax: 650-688-5889
Web: hereuare.com

Hotspotzz Inc.
265 East 100 South, Ste. 245
Salt Lake City, UT 84111
Tel: 801-415-8090
E-mail: amy@hotspotzz.com

Hewlett-Packard
3000 Hanover St.
Palo Alto, CA 94304-1185
Tel: 650-857-1501
Fax: 650-857-5518
Web: hp.com

Hyperlink Tech.
1201 Clint Moore Rd.
Boca Raton FL 33487
Tel: 561-995-2256
Fax: 561-995-2432
E-mail: sales@hyperlinktech.com

Hughes Network Systems
11717 Exploration Ln.
Germantown, MD 20876
Tel: 301-428-5500
Fax: 301-428-1868
Web: hns.com

IBM Corporation
1133 Westchester Ave.
White Plains, NY 10604
Tel: 1-800-IBM-4YOU
Web: ibm.com

IEEE
3 Park Ave., 17th Flr.
New York, NY 10016-5997
Tel: 212-419-7900
Fax: 212-752-4929
Web: ieee.org

Intel Corporation
2200 Mission College Blvd.
Santa Clara, CA 95052
Fax: 408-765-9904
Web: intel.com

Intersil Corporation Headquarters
675 Trade Zone Blvd
Milpitas, CA 95035
Tel: 408-935-4300
FAX: 408-945-9305
Web: intersil.com

iPass
3800 Bridge Parkway
Redwood Shores, CA 94065
Tel: 650-232-4100
Fax: 650-232-4111
Web: ipass.com

ITU
Place des Nations
CH-1211 Geneva 20
Switzerland
Tel: 41-22-730-51-11
E-mail: sales@itu.int

Linksys (Cisco)
17401 Armstrong Ave.
Irvine, CA 92614
Tel: 800-546-5797
Web: linksys.com

Lucent Technologies
600 Mountain Ave.
Murray Hill, NJ 07974-0636
Tel: 908-508-8080, Press 9
E-mail: execoffice@lucent.com

Luxul Corporation
905 North Main St., Ste. D1
North Salt Lake, UT 84054
Tel: 801-299-0999 Ext. 121
Fax: 801-299-0911
E-mail: tyler@luxul.net

Mesh Networks
PO Box 948133
Maitland, FL 32794
Tel: 407-659-5300
Fax: 407-659-5301
E-mail: sales@meshnetworks.com

Motia Inc.
225 Lake Ave., Ste. 710
Pasadena, CA 91101
Tel: 626-405-4435
Fax: 626-405-4436
E-mail: info@motia.com

Motorola
2900 South Diablo Way
Tempe, AZ 85282,
Tel: 800-759-1107
Web: motorola.com

MuniWireless
info@muniwireless.com

NetGear Inc.
4500 Great America Pkwy.
Santa Clara, California 95054
Tel: 408-907-8000
Fax: 408-907-8097
Web: netgear.com

NetNearU
2908 Finfeather Rd.
Bryan, TX 77801
Tel: 877-599-7253
Fax: 979-775-4393
E-mail: sales@nnu.com

Network Chemistry
1170 University Ave.
Palo Alto, CA, 94301
Tel: 650-575-1425
Fax: 253-323-9244
Web: networkchemistry.com

Newbury Networks, Inc.
745 Boylston St.
Boston, MA 02116
Tel: 617-867-7007
Fax: 617-867-7001
E-mail: info@newburynetworks.com

Nokia
Nokia Head Office
Keilalahdentie 2-4, PO Box 226
FIN-00045 Nokia Group
Finland
Tel: 358-7180-08000
Web: nokia.com

Nomadix
31355 Agoura Rd.
Westlake Village, CA 91361
Tel: 818-597-1500
E-mail: info@nomadix.com

Nortel Networks
8200 Dixie Rd., Ste. 100
Brampton, Ontario
L6T 5P6, Canada
Tel: 905-863-0000
Web: nortelnetworks.com

NYC Wireless
532 LaGuardia Place, Ste. 138
New York, NY 10012
E-mail: info@nycwireless.net

Pacific Wireless
693 E. Draper Heights Wy.
Ste. 210
Draper, UT 84020
Tel: 801-572-3024
Fax: 801-572-3025
Web: pacwireless.com

Palm
400 N. McCarthy Blvd.
Milpitas, CA 95035
Tel: 408-503-7000
Fax: 408-503-2750
Web: palm.com

Peoplesoft
4460 Hacienda Dr.
Pleasanton, CA 94588-8618
Tel: 800-380-7638
Web: peoplesoft.com

Pronto Networks
4637 Chabot Dr, Ste. 350
Pleasanton, CA 94588
Tel: 925-227-5500
Fax: 925-460-8227
E-mail: info@prontonetworks.com

Proxim
935 Stewart Dr.
Sunnyvale, CA 94085
Toll free: 800-229-1630
Tel: 408-731-2700
Fax: 408-731-3675
Web: proxim.com

Radiant Networks
The Mansion, Chesterford Park
Little Chesterford, Essex
CB10 1XL England
Tel: 44-0-1799-533-600
Fax: 44-0-1799-533-601
E-mail: support@radiantnetworks.co.uk

Rocksteady Networks
3410 Far West Blvd. Ste. 210
Austin, Texas 78731
Tel: 512-275-0571
Fax: 512-275-0575
E-mail: info@rocksteady.com

RoomLinx
6553 Via Sereno
Ranch Murieta, CA 95683
Tel: 800-576-1655
Fax: 916-354-0544
E-mail: sales@roomlinx.com

Service Factory
Årstaängsvägen 17, SE-117 43
Stockholm, Sweden
Tel: 46-8-18-00-26
Fax: 46-8-18-00-29
E-mail: info@servicefactory.com

Siemens AG
Wittelsbacherplatz 2
D-80333 Munich
Germany
Tel.: 49-89-636-00
Fax: 49-89-636-52-000
Web: siemens.com

SkyNetGlobal Ltd.
Ste. 16, 123 Liverpool St.
Sydney NSW 2000
Australia
Tel: 612-8251-3800
Fax: 612-8251-3809
E-mail: sales@skynetglobal.com

SMC
38 Tesla
Irvine, CA 92618
Tel: 800-762-4968
Fax: 949-679-1481
Web: smc.com

SONY
6-7-35 Kitashinagawa
Shinagawa-ku
Tokyo 141-0001
Japan
Web: sony.net

Surf and Sip, Inc.
470 Third St., Ste. 100
San Francisco, CA 94107
Tel: 415-974-6321
Fax: 415-777-2469
E-mail: info@surfandsip.com

SyBase
One Sybase Dr.
Dublin, CA 94568
Tel: 925-236-5000
Web: sybase.com

Symbol Technologies, Inc.
One Symbol Plaza
Holtsville, NY 11742-1300
Tel: 866-416-8545
Fax: 631-738-5990
E-mail: info@symbol.com

Telia-Sonera AB
Mårbackagatan 11
SE-123 86 Farsta
Sweden
Tel: 46-0-8-504-550-00
Fax: 46-0-8-504-550-01
E-mail: teliasonera@telia.se

Texas Instruments, Inc.
Product Information Center
13532 N. Central Expressway
M/S 3807
Dallas, Texas 75243-1108
Tel: 972-644-5580
Fax : 972-927-6377
Web: ti.com

T-Mobile
PO Box 37380
Albuquerque, NM 87176-7380
Tel: 800-937-8997
Web: t-mobile.com

Toshiba
1-1, Shibaura 1-chome, Minato-ku,
Tokyo 105-8001
Japan
Tel: 81-3-3457-4511
Fax : 81-3-3456-1631
Web: toshiba.com

Tropos Networks
1710 S. Amphlett Blvd., Ste. 304
San Mateo, CA 94402
Tel: 650-286-4250
Fax: 650-286-4259
E-mail: info@troposnetworks.com

Vivato
139 Townsend St., Ste. 200
San Francisco, CA 94107
Tel: 415-495-1111
Fax: 415-495-6430
Web: vivato.net

Wavelink
11332 NE 122nd Way, Ste. 300
Kirkland, Washington 98034
Tel: 1-888-699-9283
Fax: (425) 823-0143
E-mail: customerservice@wavelink.com

Wayport
8303 N. Mopac, Ste. A-300
Austin, TX 78759
Tel: 972-791-3900
E-mail: info@wayport.net

WiDeFi Inc.
476 A1A, Ste. 3
Satellite Beach, FL 32937
Tel: 321-777-2085
E-mail: info@WiDeFi.com

Wi-Fi Alliance
2716 Barton Creek Blvd, Ste. 2024
Austin, TX 78735
Tel: 512-347-7660
E-mail: fhanzlik@wi-fi.org

WiFi Planet
Web: wi-fiplanet.com

WiFinder
E-mail: sales@wifinder.com
Web: wifinder.com

Wild Packets Inc.
1340 Treat Blvd, Ste. 500
Walnut Creek, CA 94597
Tel: 925-937-3200
E-mail: info@wildpackets.com

WiMAX Forum
Web: wimaxforum.org

Wipro Technologies
Doddakannelli Sarjapur Rd.
Bangalore-560 035
India
Tel: 91-80-8440011
E-mail: info@wipro.com

Wireless Internet Institute
225 Franklin St., 26th Flr.
Boston, MA 02110
Tel: 617-439-5400
Fax: 617-439-5415
E-mail: daghion@w2i.org
Web: w2i.org

Xnet Wireless
PO Box 555 Mornington 3931
Australia
Tel: 03-5976-2185
E-mail: sales@x.net.au

Recommended readings

802.11 Wireless Networks: The Definitive Guide (O'Reilly Networking), by Matthew S. Gast. O'Reilly & Associates; 1st edition (April 2002). ISBN: 0596001835.

Book of Wi-Fi, The: Install, Configure, and Use 802.11b Wireless Networking, by John Ross. No Starch Press; (February 2003). ISBN: 188641145X

Brave New Women of Asia: How Distance Education Changed Their Lives, edited by Kanwar and Taplin. This report reviews the impact of distance education on women in Hong Kong, India, Pakistan, Sri Lanka, and Bangladesh. The report encourages women to participate in open and distance learning.

Bridging the Digital Divide: Gyandoot: The Model for Community Networks, by Rajesh Rajora (2002). Tata McGraw-Hill, New Delhi. This book covers theoretical models of community access, networking infrastructure, information needs assessment, user behavior, research findings and recommendations for similar projects.

Build Your Own Wi-Fi Network, by Shelly Brisbin, Glen Carty (Contributor). McGraw-Hill Osborne Media; (October 22, 2002). ISBN: 0072226242

Building Wireless Community Networks, by Rob Flickenger. O'Reilly & Associates; 1st edition (December 15, 2001). ISBN: 0596002041.

China Dawn: The Story of Technology and Business Revolution, by David Sheff (2002). Documents and investigates the Internet sector in China, as well as India, Japan and Singapore.

CWNA Certified Wireless Network Administrator Official Study Guide (Exam PW0-100), by Devin Akin. McGraw-Hill Osborne Media; 2nd edition (February 18, 2003). ISBN: 0072229020.

CWSP Certified Wireless Security Professional Official Study Guide (Exam PW0-200), by Planet3 Wireless. McGraw-Hill Osborne Media; (August 2003). ISBN: 0072230126.

Deploying License-Free Wireless Wide-Area Networks, by Jack Unger. Cisco Press; 1st edition (February 26, 2003). ISBN: 1587050692

Field Guide to Wireless LANs for Administrators and Power Users, by Thomas Maufer. Prentice Hall PTR; 1st edition (October 17, 2003). ISBN: 0131014064.

First Mile of Connectivity: Advancing Communications for Rural Development, edited by Richardson and Paisley. FAO, (1998). This book is divided into four sections: Lessons Learned from other Media and Participatory Communications Practices; Starting with the First Mile of Connectivity: Affordable, Adaptable, Profitable and Practical Rural Telephone and Telecommunications Systems; ICTs as Tools to Support Participatory Communication Initiatives for Rural and Agricultural Knowledge Systems; The Policy Context: The Keystone to Improving Rural Telecommunications and ICT Application for Development. The book is available from the website of the UN Food and Agricultural Organization.

Fixed Broadband Wireless System Design, by Harry R. Anderson. John Wiley & Sons; (February 27, 2003). ISBN: 0470844388

Maximum Wireless Security, by Cyrus Peikari and Seth Fogie. SAMS; Book and CD-ROM edition (December 18, 2002). ISBN: 0672324881

Public Wi-Fi LAN Threat Becomes Wireless Carrier Opportunity, by Yankee Group. MarketResearch.com; ISBN: B00007KSFP; (October 1, 2002).

Voice-over IP and IP Telephony: References
http://www.cis.ohio-state.edu/~jain/refs/ref_voip.htm

Wi-Fi Handbook: Building 802.11b Wireless Networks, by Konrad Roeder, Frank D., Jr. Ohrtman. McGraw-Hill Professional; (April 10, 2003). ISBN: 0071412514.

Glossary

3G—The third generation of mobile communications specified by the ITU promises to offer increased bandwidth and high-speed data applications up to 2 Mbps. It works over wireless air interfaces such as GSM, TDMA, and CDMA.

802.11 Standard—The series of wireless standards developed by the IEEE. Commonly known as Wi-Fi.

802.11a—A wireless networking specification, assigned by IEEE, in the 5-Ghz frequency range with a bandwidth of 54 Mbps.

802.11b—A wireless networking specification, assigned by IEEE, in the 2.4-Ghz frequency range with a bandwidth of 11 Mbps.

802.11g—A wireless networking specification, assigned by IEEE, in the 2.4 Ghz frequency range with a bandwidth of 54 Mbps.

802.16—A group of broadband wireless communications standards for metropolitan area networks (MANs) developed by a working group of the IEEE.

802.20—A specification of physical and medium access control layers of an air interface for interoperable mobile broadband wireless access systems, operating in licensed bands below 3.5 Ghz, optimized for IP-data transport, with peak data rates per user in excess of 1 Mbps. It supports various vehicular mobility classes up to 250 km/h in a MAN environment and targets spectral efficiencies, sustained user data rates, and numbers of active users that are all significantly higher than achieved by existing mobile systems. This standard is under development.

Access Point—A wireless hardware device connected to a wired network that enables wireless devices to connect to a wired LAN.

Ad-Hoc Mode—See **Peer-to-Peer**.

Analog—Modulated radio signals that enable transfer of information such as voice and data.

Antenna—A device used for transmitting and/or receiving radio signals, whose shape and size is determined by the frequency of signal it is receiving.

Authentication—A process of identifying a user, usually based on a username and password, ensuring that the individual is whom he or she claims to be, without saying anything about the access rights of the individual.

Backbone—The central part of a large network to which two or more subnetworks link. It is the primary path for data transmission. A network can have a wired backbone or a wireless backbone.

Bandwidth—The amount of data a network can carry, i.e., how much and how fast data flows on a given transmission path. It is measured by bits or bytes per second.

Base Station—The central radio transmitter/receiver that maintains communications with mobile radiotelephone sets within a given range (typically a cell site).

Bits per second (bps)—The number of bits that can be sent or received per second over a communication line.

Bluetooth Wireless Technology—A short-range wireless specification that allows for radio connections (2.4 Ghz) transmitting voice and data between devices (such as portable computers, personal digital assistants, or PDAs, and mobile phones) within a 30-foot range of each other.

Broadband—A fast Internet connection generally above 200 Kbps. However, no official speed definition exists for broadband services.

Cable—A broadband transmission technology using coaxial cable or fiber-optic lines that was first used for TV and is now being used for Internet access.

Channel—A path along which a communications signal is transmitted.

Client Devices—These communicate with hub devices such as access points and gateways. They include PC cards that slide into laptop computers, PCMCIA modules embedded in laptop computers, and mobile computing devices.

Client—An end user, i.e., any computer connected to a network that requests services (files, print capability), from another member of the network.

Consumer Premise Equipment (CPE)—Devices located at home or office such as telephones, PBXs, and other communication devices.

Dial-Up—A communication connection using standard copper wire telephone network.

Digital—Technology used in telecommunications where information is processed by first converting it to a stream of ones and zeros, permitting extremely complicated systems to be designed and manufactured at reasonable cost through the use of ASICs and computer circuitry while meeting very high performance standards.

DNS—A program that accesses a database on a collection of Internet servers to translate URLs to Internet packet (IP) addresses.

DSL—Various technology protocols for high-speed data, voice, and video transmission over ordinary twisted-pair copper POTS (Plain Old Telephone Service) telephone wires.

Ethernet—Also called 10Base T, Ethernet is an international standard for wired networks. It can offer a bandwidth of about 10 Mbps and up to 100 Mbps.

Firewall—Software, hardware, or a combination of the two that prevents unrestricted access into or out of a network.

Gateway—A combination of a software program and piece of hardware that passes data between networks. In wireless networking, gateways can also serve as security and authentication devices, access points, and more.

Hertz (Hz)—The unit for expressing frequency (f), a measure of electromagnetic energy. One Hertz equals one cycle per second.

Hotspot—A place where users can access Wi-Fi service for free or a fee.

Hotzone—An area where users can access Wi-Fi service free or for a fee.

Hub—A multiport device used to connect several PCs to a network.

IEEE—Institute of Electrical and Electronics Engineers (www.ieee.org), in New York, is an organization composed of engineers, scientists, and students and is best known for developing standards for the computer and electronics industry. In particular, the IEEE 802.xx standards for local-area networks are widely followed.

Internet Appliance—A computer intended primarily for Internet access, generally offering customized Web browsing, touch-screen navigation, e-mail services, entertainment, and personal information management applications.

Internet Protocol (IP)—A set of rules used to send and receive messages at the Internet address level.

IP Address—A 32-bit number that identifies each sender or receiver of information that is sent across the Internet. An IP address has two parts—an identifier of a particular network on the Internet and an identifier of the particular device (which can be a server or a workstation) within that network.

ISS—A special software application that allows all PCs on a network access to the Internet simultaneously through a single connection and Internet Service Provider (ISP) account.

Local Area Network (LAN)—A high-speed network that connects a limited number of computers in a small area, generally a building or a couple of buildings.

MAC—A unique identifier that can be used to provide security for wireless networks. All Wi-Fi devices have an individual MAC address hard-coded into it.

Mapping—Assigning a PC to a shared drive or printer port on a network.

Network Interface Card (NIC)—A type of PC adapter card that works without wires (Wi-Fi) or attaches to a network cable to provide two-way communication between the computer and network devices such as a hub or switch.

PC Card—A credit-card-sized removable peripheral that plugs into a special slot on portable computers (and some desktop models), including Wi-Fi cards, memory cards, modems, NICs, hard drives, etc.

Peer-to-Peer Network (P2P)—Also known as Ad-hoc mode, a network of computers that has no server or central hub. Each computer acts both as a client and network server. It can be either wireless or wired.

Personal Area Network (PAN)—A casual, close-proximity network where connections are made on the fly and temporarily. Meeting attendees, for example, can connect their Bluetooth-enabled notebook computers to share data across a conference-room table, but they break the connection once the meeting is over.

Personal Digital Assistant (PDA)—is a digital handheld device that is can transmit data and services such as paging, data messaging, computing, telephone/fax, email, etc. possible.

Plug and Play—A feature of a computer system which enables automatic configuration of add-ons and peripheral devices like wireless PC Cards, printers, scanners and multi-media devices.

POTS—Standard analog telephone service.

Radio Frequency (RF)—Any frequency within the electromagnetic spectrum associated with radio-wave propagation.

Range—The distance a wireless signal can reach.

Repeater—A device that receives a radio signal, amplifies it, and retransmits it in a new direction. Repeaters are used in wireless networks to extend the range of base-station signals, thereby expanding coverage—within limits—more economically than by building additional base stations.

Roaming—The ability to move from one access point coverage area to another without losing connectivity.

Satellite Broadband—A wireless high-speed Internet connection provided by satellites. Some satellite broadband connections are two-way—up and down. Others are one-way, with the satellite providing a high-speed downlink and then using a dial-up telephone connection or other land-based system for the uplink to the Internet.

Server—A computer that lets other computers and devices on a network share its resources. Includes print servers, Internet servers, and data servers. A server can also be combined with a hub or router.

Software Defined Radio (SDR)—Refers to wireless communication in which the transmitter modulation is generated or defined by a computer, and the receiver uses a computer to recover the signal intelligence.

Spectrum Allocation—The range of frequencies designated by a National Telecommunications Regulatory Authority for a category of use or uses.

Switch—A network device that selects the path that a data packet will take to its next destination ensuring optimal network performance. The switch opens and closes the electrical circuit to determine whether and to where data will flow.

TCP/IP—The underlying technology behind the Internet and communications between computers in a network. The first part, TCP, is the transport part, which matches the size of the messages on both end and guarantees that the correct message has been received. The IP part is the user's computer address on a network.

Unlicensed Spectrum—The government sets up general rules, such as the power limits on devices, and then allows any device that meets those standards to operate (unlicensed) in that spectrum.

Very Small Aperture Terminal (VSAT)—An earthbound station used in communications of data, voice, and video signals, excluding broadcast television, consisting of two parts: a transceiver placed outdoors in direct line-of-sight to the satellite, and a device placed indoors to interface the transceiver with the end user's communications device, such as a PC.

Virtual Private Network (VPN)—A private network of computers at least partially connected by public phone lines. An example is a private office LAN that allows users to log in remotely over the Internet (an open public system). VPNs use encryption and secure protocols such as PPTP to ensure that unauthorized parties do not intercept data transmissions.

Voice-Over IP (VoIP)—Technology that supports voice transmission via IP-based LANs, WANs, and the Internet.

Wide Area Network (WAN)—A network that connects computers and other devices across a large local, regional, national, or international area.

Wi-Fi Alliance—A coalition of wireless-industry leaders committed to the open inter-operability of 802.11 IEEE standards.

WiMax Forum—A coalition of wireless-industry leaders committed to the open inter-operability of all products used for broadband wireless access based on 802.16 IEEE standards.

Wireless Internet Service Provider (WISP)—An organization providing wireless access to the Internet.

Wireless Loop (WL)—A wireless system providing the "last mile" connectivity; that is, the last wired connection between the telephone exchange and the subscriber's telephone set (which can be up to several miles in length). Traditionally, this has been provided by a copper-wire connection.

Wireless—Use of radio-frequency spectrum to transmit and receive voice, data, and video signals for communications.

World Radiocommunication Conference (WRC)—An international conference organized by ITU at which standards and interference issues are discussed at the inter-governmental level.

Index

telekisoks, xvi, 32, 73-76, 79-82, 93-95, 102
telemedicine, 44, 47, 49
Telenor, 28
telephone, xiii, xiv, xv, 3, 25, 27-29, 53, 54, 57, 80, 83
Telmex, 57, 58
train station, 8, 100
Tunisia, 56
Uganda, 91
ultra wideband, 13
UMass Boston, 69-71
UN Development Program, 93-95
UN ICT Task Force, v, vii, viii, ix, xi, xv, 99
UN ICT Task Force, xi, xv, 99
Unicode, 84
UniNet Communications, 63-66
United Kingdom, 28
United Nations, v, 89, 99

United States, 1, 18, 20, 22, 25, 28, 53, 56-58, 85, 101
university, 38, 50, 63, 69-71, 73, 76, 84, 89, 102
unlicensed, 7-14, 17-22
urban areas, 3, 10, 21, 27, 28, 33, 34, 55, 60, 63, 89
USAID, 65, 69, 70
value chain, xvi, 1, 79, 107, 108, 110
Venezuela, 19
village, xv, 1, 25-28, 39, 44, 50, 55, 73-85
Virtual Yeti team, 43-45
voice-over IP, xiii, xiv, 11, 19, 39, 43, 44, 55, 58, 83, 84, 100
Voxiva, 91
VSAT, 44, 47, 79
webcam, 58
Wi-Fi Alliance, 100
Wi-Fi, v, vii, viii, xiii, xiv, 7, 21,

22, 25, 29, 31, 32, 33, 50, 60, 61, 66, 79, 85, 89, 90, 100
WiFinder, 110
WiMax Forum, 100
WiMax, xiii, xiv, 9, 100, 109
WINX, 66
Wireless Internet Exchange, 66
Wireless Internet Institute, v, vii, viii, xi, xv, 17, 37, 99, 116
WISPs, xv, 17, 18, 31, 37, 53-66, 101
WLAN, 7, 9, 11, 18, 21, 84, 93, 94
World Bank, 1, 59, 81
World Radio Conference, xiii, xiv, 8, 21, 100, 103, 109
World Summit on Information Society, xi, 37
WorldLink Communications, 43-45
Xixuaú-Xipariná Ecological Reserve, 47-50